MW00604587

Exercise for Mood and Anxiety Disorders

EDITOR-IN-CHIEF

David H. Barlow, PhD

SCIENTIFIC
ADVISORY BOARD

Anne Marie Albano, PhD

Gillian Butler, PhD

David M. Clark, PhD

Edna B. Foa, PhD

Paul J. Frick, PhD

Jack M. Gorman, MD

Kirk Heilbrun, PhD

Robert J. McMahon, PhD

Peter E. Nathan, PhD

Christine Maguth Nezu, PhD

Matthew K. Nock, PhD

Paul Salkovskis, PhD

Bonnie Spring, PhD

Gail Steketee, PhD

John R. Weisz, PhD

G. Terence Wilson, PhD

✓ **Treatments** *That Work*™

Exercise for Mood and Anxiety Disorders

Workbook

Michael W. Otto • Jasper A. J. Smits

OXFORD
UNIVERSITY PRESS

2009

OXFORD
UNIVERSITY PRESS

Oxford University Press, Inc., publishes works that further
Oxford University's objective of excellence
in research, scholarship, and education.

Oxford   New York
Auckland   Cape Town   Dar es Salaam   Hong Kong   Karachi
Kuala Lumpur   Madrid   Melbourne   Mexico City   Nairobi
New Delhi   Shanghai   Taipei   Toronto

With offices in
Argentina   Austria   Brazil   Chile   Czech Republic   France   Greece
Guatemala   Hungary   Italy   Japan   Poland   Portugal   Singapore
South Korea   Switzerland   Thailand   Turkey   Ukraine   Vietnam

Copyright © 2009 by Oxford University Press, Inc.

Published by Oxford University Press, Inc.
198 Madison Avenue, New York, New York 10016

www.oup.com

Oxford is a registered trademark of Oxford University Press

All rights reserved. No part of this publication may be reproduced,
stored in a retrieval system, or transmitted, in any form or by any means,
electronic, mechanical, photocopying, recording, or otherwise,
without the prior permission of Oxford University Press.

ISBN 978-0-19-538226-6 Paper

Printed in the United States of America
on acid-free paper

About Treatments *ThatWork*™

One of the most difficult problems confronting patients with various disorders and diseases is finding the best help available. Everyone is aware of friends or family who have sought treatment from a seemingly reputable practitioner, only to find out later from another doctor that the original diagnosis was wrong or the treatments recommended were inappropriate or perhaps even harmful. Most patients, or family members, address this problem by reading everything they can about their symptoms, seeking out information on the Internet, or aggressively "asking around" to tap knowledge from friends and acquaintances. Governments and healthcare policymakers are also aware that people in need don't always get the best treatments—something they refer to as "variability in healthcare practices."

Now healthcare systems around the world are attempting to correct this variability by introducing "evidence-based practice." This simply means that it is in everyone's interest that patients get the most up-to-date and effective care for a particular problem. Healthcare policymakers have also recognized that it is very useful to give consumers of healthcare as much information as possible, so that they can make intelligent decisions in a collaborative effort to improve health and mental health. This series, Treatments *ThatWork*™, is designed to accomplish just that. Only the latest and most effective interventions for particular problems are described in user-friendly language. To be included in this series, each treatment program must pass the highest standards of evidence available, as determined by a scientific advisory board. Thus, when individuals suffering from these problems or their family members seek out an expert clinician who is familiar with these interventions and decides that they are appropriate, they will have confidence that they are receiving the best care available. Of course, only your health care professional can decide on the right mix of treatments for you.

If you are in therapy for a mood or anxiety disorder, your treatment can be augmented with exercise and physical activity. Research has proven that individuals who exercise regularly have less stress, less anxiety, less depression, and less substance use problems than those who don't. Studies have also shown that exercise can help combat the effects of depression and anxiety.

This workbook is structured to help you prevent mood disturbances from blocking the very activities that can help you feel better. In addition to information on how to start and maintain an exercise program, this workbook comes complete with worksheets and logs for scheduling and tracking your physical activity. The information provided will help you to establish and maintain healthy exercise habits. The goal of the program described is for you to achieve some of the natural and powerful mood benefits of exercise.

David H. Barlow, Editor-in-Chief,
Treatments *ThatWork*™
Boston, MA

Dedication

MWO: To Jenni, for the laughter and joy she brings

JAJS: To Jill and Stella, for many happy exercise sessions

Acknowledgments

Our writing of the therapist guide and workbook for *Exercise for Mood and Anxiety Disorders* was motivated by research showing the tremendous benefits of exercise for mental health and well-being. We want to acknowledge the valuable evidence provided by international teams of researchers who documented these benefits in population-based studies, experimental investigations, clinical studies, meta-analytical comparisons, and review articles. We would also like to thank our collaborators on our own investigations in this area. In particular, our collaborators on research and review articles included Evi Behar, Angie Berry, Tim Church, Lynette Craft, Daniel Galper, Dina Gordon, Tracy Greer, Pamela Handelsman, Bridget Hearon, Kristin Julian, Kate McHugh, Alicia Meuret, Heather Murray, Mark Powers, Katherine Presnell, David Rosenfield, Anke Seidel, Georgia Stathopoulou, Candyce Tart, Madhukar Trivedi, and Michael Zvolensky. All of these individuals helped expand what is known about the benefits of exercise for mood and anxiety disorders.

Contents

Chapter 1

About This Workbook

Goals

- To learn about this program
- To identify the symptoms you want to address
- To select your support team
- To work with your clinician and physician to decide on your level of activity

Overview

This workbook is designed to help you structure and maintain an exercise program to improve your mood. The use of exercise for mental health is supported by a wealth of research evidence. It is clear from large-scale surveys that individuals who exercise have less stress, less anxiety, less depression, and less substance use problems than those who don't exercise. More importantly, studies show that a program of exercise can be used to treat depression and can achieve results that rival those provided by the use of antidepressant medication or psychotherapy. Likewise, programmed exercise has been found to be useful for the management of anxiety problems, including the treatment of panic disorder. This workbook will provide you with information about the program as you work with your clinician. The goal is for you to achieve some of the natural and powerful mood benefits of exercise.

In addition to information on how to start and maintain an exercise program, this workbook has specific sections relevant to the treatment of mood and anxiety disorders. It is recommended that you begin by reading and working through Chapters 1 through 4, which discuss common issues and solutions relevant for planning an exercise program. Starting, maintaining, and supplementing your exercise program is the focus of Chapters 5 through 7. Specific modifications to your exercise program relevant to depression and anxiety disorders are discussed in Chapters 8 through 10. The final chapter discusses additional strategies for maintaining an anxiety program over the long term. An appendix provides additional monitoring forms to help you stay on track with an exercise program and its benefits.

Why a Formal Treatment Program for Exercise

You probably already know that regular exercise is good for your mood and good for your body. Nonetheless, it can be hard to start or maintain an exercise program, particularly when feeling depressed or anxious. This workbook is structured to help you prevent mood disturbances from blocking the very activities that can help you feel better.

Subsequent chapters introduce ways to plan an exercise program and strategies for following through with your exercise goals. The assumption is that during this program, your mood will get in the way of naturally *feeling like* exercising. For this reason, this workbook gives you tips to make it easier to start the habit of regular exercise. It also offers ways of thinking about, scheduling, and monitoring your exercise program to help you feel the benefits and keep motivated for continued exercise.

But I Have Been *Trying* to Exercise

Exercising for mood benefits is very different from exercising for general health. When you exercise for general health, you have to work *now* to get general health benefits *later*. And when you feel sad, stressed, or anxious, it is very hard to do something in the present for the purpose of a future health benefit. However, if the goal of exercising is to stop feeling bad *now*, it becomes much easier to follow through with exercise despite having a negative mood. Over time, exercise can become the activity that you do because you want comfort and a mood lift. The fact that you also get in good shape and better your physical health is just an extra benefit. This program asks you to exercise to feel good, and because of this, feeling bad is never a reason to skip exercise. Feeling bad now *is* the very reason to exercise today!

One of the first things you will do in this program is clarify your motivations for starting an exercise program. Exercise should be a personally rewarding activity for you. In the space provided, review and identify some of the symptoms you want to address with your exercise program.

Symptoms to Be Targeted By Exercise

Please check off the mood symptoms you are targeting.

Symptoms of Depression:

_____ Sad or blue mood

_____ Loss of interest in things you care about

_____ Feelings of guilt about things done or not done

_____ Low energy and difficulties being motivated to start or finish activities

_____ Poor concentration

_____ Disrupted appetite or loss of interest in eating

_____ Feelings of agitation or lethargy

_____ Feelings that nothing matters

_____ Difficulties sleeping or poor sleep quality (or oversleeping)

Symptoms of Anxiety

_____ General anxiety

_____ Worry

_____ Feelings of anticipation

_____ Feeling jumpy

_____ Startling easily

_____ Panic attacks

_____ Avoidance of situations (write in situations:)

_____ Poor concentration

_____ Problems with sleep

_____ Feeling tense

_____ General feelings of stress

Other Symptoms You Want to Target

_____

_____

_____

As mentioned, exercise also has a wide variety of benefits other than management of mood or anxiety disorders. We also want you to be aware of these benefits and check off those you care more about.

Frequent exercise can help me to:

_____ Manage weight   _____ Enhance strength and endurance
_____ Lower cholesterol   _____ Reduce risk of heart disease
_____ Lower hypertension   _____ Enhance immune functioning
_____ Prolong life span

Again, this program doesn't ask you to exercise just because of these longer-term health benefits. It wants you to exercise to feel good *now*. Nonetheless, know that when you exercise for mood, not only are you likely to feel better, you are likely to have better health and a longer life span.

Considering Your Support Team

Because exercise may be a new habit for you, you will want to have a support team. Consider who you might want to encourage you or participate with you in your new exercise program. Take a few moments to think about who will be most supportive of your goal to develop an exercise habit. Then, consider how exercise might change your social life. Are there people with whom you would like to exercise, or are there additional social activities that you might pursue because you will be in better shape? Select members of your support team and list them in the space provided.

Also, keep in mind that your general levels of energy and comfort when engaging in activities may increase as you achieve your exercise goals. Chapter 7 of this workbook has you consider additional pleasant activities that may support you in this new lifestyle.

Selecting Members of Your Support Team

Who would be happy that you are exercising and might encourage you in this program?

_____   _____

_____   _____

_____   _____

Who might you select for support, because they have an important impact on your life?

_____   _____

_____   _____

_____   _____

Who might you want to have join you in your new exercise habit—by being with these people during exercise or seeing them after exercise?

_____   _____

_____   _____

_____   _____

Working With Your Clinician

This workbook is designed for use in conjunction with a program of exercise supervised by a clinician (a psychologist, physician, nurse, social worker, or therapist). Your clinician should play an active role in deciding if this exercise program is for you. Some clinicians will recommend exercise after you have tried medications or psychotherapy as a way to manage you mood or stress levels. Others will recommend exercise as a first step in helping you manage your mood. Regardless of the timing of this exercise intervention, know that you have a wide variety of choices in getting help for your mood, anxiety, or stress levels. No single treatment works for everyone. Cognitive-behavioral therapy, general psychotherapy, medications, or stress management programs can all provide benefits. As a good consumer, consider these options in conjunction with exercise as is needed for you to reach your mood management goals.

Knowing Your Physical Limitations

You should undergo a full medical evaluation with your physician before starting an exercise program. It is important to know your current level of physical health and to be aware of any physical conditions that should limit your participation in exercise. Let your physician know that you are about to start an exercise program that is targeting the public health recommended dose for adults from the American College of Sports Medicine and the American Heart Association. Depending on your level of fitness, you may work up to this level slowly. In addition, please make sure to have a detailed discussion with your physician if you have problems with chest pain, breathing difficulties, light-headedness, bone or joint pain, or high blood pressure, or if you are taking medications for a heart condition or high blood pressure. Even with these conditions, this exercise program might be right for you, but the decision about your level of activity should be made in consultation with your physician.

Chapter 2 — *How Exercise Works on Mood and Anxiety*

Goals

- To learn about how exercise works to help mood

- To understand the importance of moderation

- To recognize the limitations of exercise in managing mood

- To consider other treatment options as warranted

Overview

As pointed out in the introduction to this workbook, there is now a wealth of evidence that exercise is a useful treatment for low mood and depression, with increasing evidence for similar benefits for anxiety disorders. However, although it is certain that exercise has clear benefits for mental and physical health, it is much less clear why these effects occur. The following pages outline some of the current perspectives on why exercise may act as a useful antidepressant and as a useful way to treat some anxiety conditions. Knowing the potential source of action (or actions) of exercise can help you maximize these aspects of your exercise program.

The Neurotransmitter Serotonin

Research on biological changes associated with regular exercise has shown that exercise leads to changes in some of the same neurotransmitters targeted by antidepressant medications used to treat both mood and anxiety disorders. The broad action of exercise on both of these conditions is consistent with the broad action of these medications. One way in which exercise may work is by stimulating the brain chemical (neurotransmitter) serotonin. Serotonin is an important neurotransmitter for the regulation of emotion and is the main neurotransmitter affected by medication such as Paxil®, Prozac®, Zoloft®, and Celexa®. These medications lead to the stimulation of neurons sensitive to serotonin. Exercise, on the other hand, is associated with more directly raising serotonin levels, as judged by studies of exercise among animals.

Stress and Sleep Management

In addition to more direct effects on neurotransmitters involved in the regulation of mood, exercise may also have indirect effects on mood through the normalization of sleep patterns. Sleep problems have been implicated in either the onset or maintenance of both mood and anxiety disorders. Medication treatments of these conditions often improve sleep, and likewise there is evidence that exercise can improve sleep as well. Since sleep normalization is important for both support of your exercise habits and mood, Chapter 7 is devoted to additional discussion of good sleep habits.

The post-exercise period may also be important for achieving broader mood benefits from exercise. The feelings of relaxation, well-being, and accomplishment that can follow a successful exercise episode may be significant in further calming anxiety and easing depression. During this time, a person may be less likely to be affected by some of the negative thinking patterns of depression, making it easier after exercise to view the next several hours in a more positive light. Even a few hours relief from feelings of depression or anxiety may work like a crowbar to give leverage for moving away the full syndrome of these disorders. For this reason, try to be particularly mindful of the benefits of exercise in the hours after an exercise episode. This will help enhance your desire to exercise on the following day, but may also play an important role in driving away negative mood states.

Also, the beneficial effects of exercise on reducing feelings of stress may have importance for *prevention* of both mood and anxiety disorders. Stressful events challenge mood, and in a number of studies, stress has been linked to relapse in depressive or anxiety disorders. To the extent that exercise can help you manage feelings of stress, it can help you prevent the onset or relapse of these disorders.

Activity Levels

As will be discussed in Chapters 8 through 10, many of the disorders that exercise can be used to treat are characterized by self-perpetuating cycles that involve low activity or avoidance. Exercise may work in part because it returns the body to adaptive action. It is also expected to increase your resilience to negative mood states. As you learn to exercise independently of the way you feel, the meaning of your negative emotions might change. Sad or anxious feelings may start to feel less overwhelming. Moreover, as you stay active despite low moods, these episodes of mood should last less time.

Reductions in Concerns About Symptoms

In addition, exercise can also have some powerful effects on how bodily sensations, including the experience of emotion, are interpreted. In particular, Chapter 10 introduces you to the most common patterns that underlie panic disorder. Of these, the most important pattern is the degree to which fears and concerns about the somatic sensations of anxiety can amplify your emotional experience. This *fear-of-fear* cycle not only predisposes individuals toward panic attacks, but also appears to make a wide variety of situations more difficult to tolerate. For example, when people fear sensations of anxiety, it is harder to quit smoking, because the sensations of withdrawal and craving from nicotine abstinence are harder to tolerate. The result is people with fears of anxiety sensations fail their quit attempt more quickly than those without those fears. The same appears to be true for tolerating other sensations, such as the shortness of breath from asthma and the heart palpitations that some individuals feel when anxious.

In short, when people fear bodily symptoms, it becomes harder to tolerate these sensations no matter what their source. It has been found that exercise can reduce these fears of anxiety sensations. This means that exercise can be used as a general tool to help individuals to be less pushed around by the sensations they experience. When you become more comfortable with your own experience of anxiety, it will be easier for you to choose how to react to anxiety sensations, rather than feel like anxiety is choosing your actions for you.

Moderation

It is important to keep a balance of exercise and rest, with attention to giving your body the moderation it needs to promote mood stability. This theme is directly addressed in Chapter 9, which discusses the application of exercise to the comanagement of bipolar disorder. The direct antidepressant effects of exercise, along with normalizing your sleep, balancing the sleep–wake cycle, and achieving a balanced schedule of activity may be helpful in calming some of the depressed mood and unstable mood that is at the heart of bipolar disorder. Also, because some of the pharmacological treatments for bipolar disorder have the side effect of weight gain, the effects of regular exercise on weight control may be an additional appealing aspect of this program for individuals with bipolar disorder.

What Exercise Does Not Treat

Using exercise to help manage mood and anxiety disorders does *not* mean you should ignore other treatment options. There is ample evidence that certain types of psychotherapy and medication treatment options are effective for treating mood and anxiety disorders. Exercise can be considered as a complement to these approaches or can be tried on its own. If you don't achieve the results you desire with this program, a consultation to consider other treatment approaches is strongly recommended. And, at every point, it is important for you to be a good consumer of treatment options.

Use of exercise to dampen stress is not a substitute for the use of good problem-solving skills. Likewise, the use of exercise to change how you react to emotions is not a substitute for fuller examination of emotional patterns in your life. For example, along with exercise to reduce the effects of stress, you may need to plan how to better manage the stressors in your life. Aim to always strike a balance between considering what your body needs and using the body to calm the mind, while also making sure that you use all the resources you can to aid your mood management. This is especially true if you have serious worsening of symptoms or ever have suicidal thoughts. Suicidal thoughts are a symptom of depression and it is important that you treat such thoughts as a symptom *in need of immediate treatment*. Any thoughts of self-injury should be discussed with a qualified clinician.

Exercise and Psychotherapy

Your mind and body are connected, and in this exercise program, you are intervening with the body to help the mind and mood. As such, exercise is an especially fitting complement to psychotherapy. To balance the focus in psychotherapy on talking, understanding, feeling, and planning, exercise helps keep you focused on doing, moving, and achieving. Exercise will help you establish healthy patterns of activity and rest, with a balance of each.

This program aims to help you provide treatment to yourself—to give yourself what your body needs to help your mind and emotions stay in balance. As part of being an informed consumer, more information on the nature and treatment of mood and anxiety disorders can be obtained from the National Institute of Mental Health on the Web site at www.nimh.nih.gov/health/topics/.

Chapter 3   *Breaking Barriers to Exercise*

Goals

- To learn how to motivate yourself by taking steps *toward* exercise

- To choose a time to exercise in your daily schedule

- To plan for exercise (clothes, music, route, etc.)

- To research online and local resources (optional)

- To find an exercise partner or group (optional)

Overview

Starting a new program of regular exercise is challenging. Everyday life events, hassles, and bad habits can interfere with your best intentions. The good news is that many of these obstacles are predictable, understandable, and avoidable. In this chapter, you will be introduced to some of the situational factors that can interfere with establishing a program of regular exercise. Also, you will start becoming familiar with interventions for these patterns and how to construct situations to help support your exercise goals.

Motivation

A useful starting point in considering barriers to exercise is to consider the concept of MOTIVATION. Motivation is frequently assumed to be a stable inward trait that precedes behavior change and helps determine the success of your goals and intentions. This is not necessarily true. A strong motivation to change does not always precede useful behavior change. This is because the desire to do something often follows the successful completion of the behavior. It is by doing something one or more times that one can establish the inward desire (the motivation) to do it again. As such, it is not expected for you to have a strong feeling that exercise is important at the beginning of this program. That feeling may well come *after* you have successfully altered your mood, anxiety, or stress through exercise.

Changing Conditions to Enhance Motivation

Because motivation can follow rather than precede useful habits, it is crucial to make new habits easy enough to start and maintain rather than just hope for motivation. This brings us to the second point: feelings of motivation are richly dependent on the external environment as well as your current thoughts and mood. The key is to make changes in your environment in order to enhance your motivation. In short, rather than simply expecting yourself to feel like exercising, this program will have you *arrange the conditions* so you will more naturally feel like exercising.

Consider the following situation. When coming home from work, and finally getting a chance to sit down and relax, it can be overwhelming to think about getting back up and completing a workout. At these moments, it is important to realize that, from the vantage point of the couch, getting up and going to the gym is really hard. The key is not to overwhelm yourself with such hard expectations. All you need to do is put yourself in the condition where going to the gym or doing some form of exercise is a more natural thought. So, instead of focusing on getting yourself to exercise, *focus only on the next step* that will make it more likely that you will exercise. For example, from the position of being on the couch, the first goal is helping yourself take one step toward being ready for exercise, such as putting on your workout clothes. Figure 3.1 illustrates this process.

Now think about situations where you might "get stuck" trying to get yourself to exercise. Record them in the space provided. For many people, the topmost difficult situation might be television time, where it is easy to think, "let me just sit here for a while longer."

_____

_____

_____

_____

_____

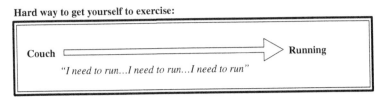

Hard way to get yourself to exercise:

Couch ⟹ Running

"*I need to run...I need to run...I need to run*"

Easier way to get yourself to exercise

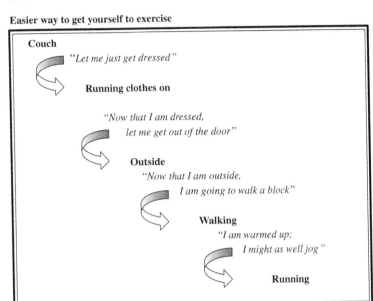

Couch

"*Let me just get dressed*"

Running clothes on

"*Now that I am dressed,
let me get out of the door*"

Outside

"*Now that I am outside,
I am going to walk a block*"

Walking

"*I am warmed up;
I might as well jog*"

Running

Figure 3.1

Setting the Stage for Exercise Success

Next, try to identify a few things that might help you get off the couch and exercise. Remember that the only goal is to have you change the situation (and how you are currently thinking and feeling) enough to make it more likely that you will exercise. Here are a few suggestions:

- Change into your workout clothes.

- Decide to do 10 sit-ups on the floor or some brief stretching while you are deciding whether to exercise.

- Go to the bathroom and look at your eyes in the mirror and discuss with your reflection whether you want to exercise.

- Think of the good music you might listen to while exercising and go get your music player.

- Daydream about how it will feel when you are done exercising.

- Remember how good you felt when you exercised last.

- Call a friend and see if she wants to exercise.

- Get out this workbook and review a chapter.

- Get yourself a glass of ice water to prepare (hydrate) for exercise.

- Remind yourself that a bad mood is a reason to exercise, not a reason to skip exercise.

- Remind yourself that starting your exercise is often the most difficult part of your exercise routine; once you start, it will get easier.

Write your own ideas in the space provided:

_____

_____

_____

_____

_____

Making It Easier to Exercise: Timing

To avoid exercise feeling like a battle of motivations, consider ways of setting up your exercise schedule so that it will fit your lifestyle and maximize your urge to exercise. The following sections are designed to help you think about some of the factors that can be important in the process of making it easier to exercise, starting with the timing of your exercise.

When it comes to supporting a new exercise habit, first think through some of the situational and timing factors that may make it easier to start and maintain your exercise program. That is, when you schedule exercise, it can make a big difference for how well you complete it. If possible, schedule exercise around natural breaks in your day and for when it is likely to make you feel best. Also, because exercise typically involves a change of clothes and, in many cases, a shower afterwards, it is important to plan how these disruptions fall into your daily routine.

Morning Exercise

Some individuals select morning exercise as a way to start the day. Advantages include the following:

- Exercise is an excellent way to start the day

- The exercise shower becomes the morning daily shower

- Morning time may allow more optimal weather conditions

- Early morning time is excellent "*me*" time

- All day you get to enjoy the sense of accomplishment of having already exercised

Challenges to morning exercise include *difficulties getting out of bed for exercise.* Because most people are limited on time because of work, school, or home demands in the morning, delays in getting out of bed can seriously interfere with morning exercise time. Also, early in the morning—when you are only half awake—it is difficult to make decisions. Make the decision about whether you are going to exercise before going to bed. Then stick to this decision. Be careful of motivation-sapping thoughts such as the following:

- *I will skip my workout just this one time.*

- *It is too cold to get out of bed.*

- *It will be more valuable for my mood if I sleep in.*

- *Missing my workout once won't matter.*

Beware of delaying tactics that close out or substantially reduce your exercise time. Remember that you made your decision to exercise when you had an *awake mind* the previous evening. Don't let any of the following thoughts have power to push you away from exercising (and these thoughts do have lots of power for a half-awake mind):

- *I will just turn over in bed one more time before I get up.*

- *Staying in bed 10 more minutes won't matter.*

- *I am too tired to exercise well.*

- *I can always exercise this evening.*

Anticipating your reactions the night before your exercise may help you counter your arguments against starting exercise the next morning. Having these thoughts hit you in the morning may then even bring a smile to your face and motivate you to get started.

Afternoon Exercise

An afternoon exercise break is an excellent strategy for stress management. It can make use of a segmented day (e.g., the long lunch and break before a return to work that is so popular in European countries). With a fixed mid-day break for exercise, the work day can lose its marathon quality. There is the morning work routine, and then a break in which the levels of stress are reduced. During this break, the body gets to be active and the mind gets to rest. Then, one can return to the afternoon physically tired but mentally refreshed and ready to meet home, work, school, or personal goals. One of the major challenges to getting out for the mid-day exercise break is the tendency to *one more thing* yourself away from having time to exercise. Thoughts characterizing this "one more thing" tendency include the following:

- *I am working well; I will get just one more thing done.*

- *I am too busy. I better not take a break till later.*

- *If I don't finish this now, it will be too overwhelming later.*

To counter these motivation-sapping thoughts, you will need to remind yourself that exercise may enhance your problem-solving levels while reducing your stress. You may be physically tired after exercise, but your productivity may shoot up due to having a clear and refreshed mind. So to counter the above "one more thing" thoughts, you may want to remind yourself:

- *I am taking a break to exercise to have a fresh mind for my afternoon job demands.*

- *I know that I feel different after exercise; let me see what work feels like under those conditions.*

- *Management of my stress and mood is one way I am helping myself be more productive.*

Evening Exercise

Evening exercise can be a terrific way to close out the day and prepare for an especially relaxed and enjoyable end to your day. Some people use evening exercise as a way to close out the work day and reduce stress prior to being with family or friends. Others may be able to incorporate a run into their commute home or use exercise and the post-exercise shower and change of clothes as their way to prepare for an enjoyable evening. The change in focus brought by exercise and a post-exercise shower can be useful for enhancing your interpersonal interactions. For example, it can help you shift your attention to the joys that can be found at home or in your social life rather than hurrying off and bringing the day's residue of work with you.

Exercising approximately 3 hours before sleep is also a good way to give yourself time to recover from exercise and take advantage of some of the natural sedating properties of a good workout.

One of the challenges of evening exercise is that you may need to cope with exercise avoidance due to fatigue from the day. Motivation-sapping thoughts include:

- *I am too tired. I can just put it off until morning.*

- *It is about to get dark.*

- *It will be too cold.*

To help you resist such thoughts, be careful with how you manage your surroundings. If you go home and sit on the couch, the likelihood that you will get back up and exercise is greatly reduced. Consider how you can exercise right after work or school. Alternatively, see if you can integrate exercise into the family routine. Jogging strollers are a terrific intervention for the busy parent who still wants to exercise. The child in the stroller may be lulled to sleep or may entertain you with conversation while you walk, jog, or run.

Planning Your Exercise

Besides timing, there are several other factors you might want to consider in planning your exercise.

Clothes and Music

Wearing comfortable clothes and dressing appropriately for the weather (with care toward protecting against being too hot or too cold) can make a big difference in your enjoyment of exercise. Also because exercise can heat the body so well, you may find that you have to layer your clothes, perhaps taking off a jacket and tying it around your waist as you complete the initial minutes of exercise.

Also, exercising with music can greatly increase the joy of exercise. For example, both of the authors of this workbook are deeply committed to running while listening to music or the local National Public Radio station. Running in time to a song, or losing oneself in the information presented on a news program, is an excellent way to enhance enjoyment while exercising. However, some care needs to be taken when wearing headphones to avoid dangerous situations; sounds of passing cars, bikes, and rollerbladers can be blocked by loud music. Be sure to take extra care (e.g., exercising with just one earphone in place) when exercising in busy areas.

The selection of exercise clothes and exercise music can form a pleasant reward for good exercise habits. Many of the clothes available in sport stores have amazing properties to allow air exchange and wick away moisture, while also providing protection from the cold. Investment in clothes that make you feel good can help support your exercise habit. Likewise, investment in good headphones and a way to carry your sound device (clips, handhelds, etc.) can help make exercise more pleasurable.

Planning Your Route

Especially early on in your exercise training program, planning your running/jogging/walking route beforehand may help you mentally prepare for your exercise session. Consider using distance markers (e.g., intersection, post office, and school) to help you break up your activity into smaller parts that are each characterized by a feeling state (e.g., hard, smooth, struggle, and easy). For example, that first section from your house to the traffic light may always be the most challenging part of your run—you are still a bit stiff and your muscles may feel tight. However, once you get to the traffic light, you have warmed up and hitting the pavement feels much better. Anticipating a difficult beginning that has an end and will be followed by a segment during which you feel much better will likely increase your motivation to get started. The authors of this workbook use the free mapping service offered by MapMyRun (http://www.mapmyrun.com) to plan their running activities.

Tracking Your Heart Rate

Consider purchasing a heart rate monitor. These simple-to-use and relatively cheap devices help you to track the fluctuation in your heart rate during exercise, which will guide you in setting and modifying intensity. These devices also allow you to estimate your average exercise-session heart rate, which will help you determine whether you are receiving the recommended exercise dose (see Chapter 5).

Exercise Partners

Finally, exercise partners can be invaluable in helping you keep up a regular exercise schedule. Refer back to the list of your support team in Chapter 1 to consider who might be a good exercise partner. This partner need not accompany you on many of your workouts; even a weekly partner can provide you with the extra support and change-up from your regular patterns to help establish an interesting and fun exercise habit.

Other Support Systems

A number of local clubs or programs may be available to support your exercise habit. For example, USA FIT is a commercial exercise support network that may be available in your city. USA FIT helps people prepare to complete exercise goals (e.g., completing a half marathon) by providing them with a training program complete with coaching, moral support, and connections to others with similar training goals. FitLink and MapMyRun are other services that provide connections to others, including information on workouts and motivational issues experienced by others. They also give users the ability to create personal profiles online, track workout results, and search for exercise partners. Both of these services share in common a Web-based approach to helping you network with and feel more connected to others in your exercise efforts. Because the quality and nature of services on the Web can change over time, be a good consumer and check the following and other links with an eye toward making sure the services are right for you.

- USA FIT: http://www.usafit.com

- FitLink: http://www.fitlink.com

- MapMyRun: http://www.mapmyrun.com.

Other resources that may be available in your area include running clubs, walking clubs, biking clubs, and, of course, workout gyms. Local sporting good stores are often a good resource for identifying clubs in your area. Drop by the store and ask the salesperson about groups that may be available in your area. It can't be overestimated how much easier it is to exercise when you have people expecting you to exercise with them.

Chapter 4   *Thinking Strategies for Exercise*

Goals

- To observe your thoughts and redirect them as needed

- To practice helpful thinking strategies *during* exercise

- To practice helpful thinking strategies *after* exercise

- To practice helpful thinking strategies *hours after* exercise

Overview

One powerful tool you have in helping yourself keep up with your exercise habit is to actively manage your thinking patterns. Thoughts can have a powerful effect in influencing mood and can either boost or sap motivation. Specific attention is given to the role of negative thoughts in mood and anxiety disorders in Chapters 8 through 10. This chapter reviews strategies for thinking about exercise in a useful way.

Enjoying the Present

So much thinking is future- and past-oriented. How has the day/week/month gone so far? What needs to be done next hour? What needs to be done next week? With all this thinking, it is often hard to realize what is going on in the moment or to be engaged enough in the moment to enjoy it. Exercise will naturally help you bring your attention back to the moment, but we want to make sure that you are ready to enjoy this effect. Indeed, one useful feature of exercise is that it is difficult to maintain worry or ruminative thinking (repetitive negative thinking) during exercise. Exercise can help individuals develop the "quiet mind" that is at the heart of many meditative techniques. Rather than thinking, monitoring, reviewing, and rehashing, the goal is to simply *experience* the current moment.

To become better at experiencing though, it is helpful to become more adept at noticing your current thinking habits.

Observing Your Thoughts

In preparation for getting the most out of exercise-related changes in cognitions, it will be important to become a good observer of the nature and content of your thoughts. To help you learn about your thinking patterns, pick a regular event that you can use as a signal for you to observe your own thinking. It can be any regularly occurring event, like the ringing of an hourly wristwatch chime, each time you open the front door to leave the house, or each time you open the refrigerator to start preparing a snack or meal. You can use these events to cue you to stop and notice whether your thoughts are present, past, or future-oriented.

Remembering to Check Your Thoughts

One of the authors' favorite events for thought observing is stoplights—that is, when waiting for a red light to change, examine ("listen in on") your thoughts. Next time you drive and are at a stoplight (see it ahead of you—red), ask yourself, "What am I thinking about right now? Where am I directing my mental energies?"

At a red light, you have the opportunity to do any of a number of pleasant activities: actively listen to the radio, hum a tune, daydream about a recent pleasant event, or plan an enjoyable event or interaction for the evening. If you find you are doing one of those things, good for you. But many readers will find they are doing none of these things; they are instead ruminating about problems—potential problems, past problems, future problems, non-existent problems—or focusing on the traffic or on the stoplight itself ("why won't you change!"). None of these topics add pleasure to your life, yet you may discover this is where you are devoting your mental energies.

Redirecting Thoughts

Try to use stoplights as your chance to start changing these patterns. When at a stoplight, notice where your thoughts go, observe the effect they have on you, and then redirect them to a more pleasurable or useful topic. You may even want to continue to think about a problem, but make sure that it is active problem solving, not just thinking about the negative aspects of a situation. With regular stoplight practice (and practice with your wristwatch chime, front door, refrigerator door, etc.), you will have a better sense of where your thoughts tend to go and more experience with gently redirecting them. Again, the task is to:

1. Notice your thoughts.

2. Observe how these thoughts make you feel

3. Redirect the thoughts to a more useful or pleasurable topic.

By learning about the nature of thinking, and becoming more adept at observing and redirecting thoughts, you will be more prepared to make use of your exercise program. That is, you will be better able to take advantage of exercise's effect of decreasing mental ruminations and to avoid some of the bad habits associated with exercise.

Thinking Strategies During Exercise

The ultimate goal for exercise is to have your thoughts centered on the present, and, if possible, on the most pleasurable aspects of your exercise session. If running outside, for example, this will include noticing the look of nature (sky, trees, color of grass, shadings of snow), interesting sights and surroundings (other people, buildings), pleasant daydreams, or the sound of music. If running inside, you may need to focus on daydreaming, music, or the sights and sounds of the gym.

Redirecting Negative Thoughts

In contrast to attention to the pleasurable aspects of running and your surroundings, it is sometimes easy to become focused on negative thoughts about running, which seems to recur with every step:

▪ *When will I be done? When will I be done? When will I be done?*

▪ *I don't like this. I don't like this. I don't like this.*

If you find yourself engaged in these bad habits, gently redirect your thinking, using gentle coaching with thoughts such as:

▪ *Ooh. This sort of thinking and attention isn't helping me. What else can I daydream about that might be more fun?*

- *When will I be done? Let me focus on what is interesting during the run. Let me take a good look at the view.*

- *I have not been listening to my music. How can thinking about being done be more interesting than this song? Let me refocus my efforts and feel my body run and enjoy running to the music.*

Expecting but Not Caring About Sensations

Chapter 10 offers additional specific strategies for dealing with concerns about or an overfocus on the symptoms of exertion, but at this point there is a simple message: Feel the sensations of exercising, but don't get stuck paying attention *only* to these sensations. When you run, your heart will pound, you will sweat, your face may flush, your body may get hot, and you may have a wide variety of aches and pains in addition to feelings of fatigue. Expect to feel these sensations. When you get good at exercising, these sensations won't go away, but you will just no longer care about them. Given that this *not caring about* (or even looking forward to) these sensations is the endpoint of a good exercise habit, you might as well begin practicing this ability now. When you exercise, be open to a wide range of experiences. Notice your feelings of breathlessness, notice the color of the tree off to your right, notice the sounds around you, notice the feel of your running stride, notice what you are daydreaming about, and keep running.

The limit to this approach is actually attending to pains or signs of injury. If there is a pebble in your shoe or your shoe laces are pinching, stop and correct the problem. If you feel you are having a knee problem or are experiencing odd muscle weakness or chest pain, consult a physician. The aim is to get good at tolerating everyday signs of exertion while also taking care of your body. Be sure to get answers to any questions you may have about odd or painful sensations or experiences during exercising.

Thoughts Immediately After Exercising

What you say to yourself after exercising will make a big difference in maintaining your exercise habit.

Rehearsal of Benefit

Exercising for a half an hour may have been hard, but it is important to ask yourself what was useful about it and to notice how you feel immediately afterwards (underscoring for yourself any immediate mood benefits). This sort of rehearsal of benefit is important for almost any situation requiring effort. Think of a work or school project where you had to apply yourself, push yourself, or otherwise put effort into finishing it. Recall the sense of relief and joy you may have felt at the completion. This joy, and making sure you feel it and remember it, is a primary factor in determining whether you feel motivated and competent the next time you need to do something hard.

Enjoying Your Success

Because exercising can be hard some days, and is at least taxing most days, you will need to make sure that you enjoy your successful exercise sessions each time they occur. Right after exercise, as you cool down, change clothes, or shower, we want you to mark your success by saying something like the following:

- *Wow, I did it.*

- *That was hard and now I feel tired but good.*

- *I am tired, but I did something really useful for my mood.*

- *I attended to my body today, and my body carried me through this run.*

- *Good for me. I walked some, I ran some, but I exercised for a full half hour.*

- *That was really hard; I really gave myself quite a workout. I can look forward to feeling the benefits of this later.*

- *I was unable to keep running. But the good news is, whether I ran or walked, I completed my 30 minutes of exercise.*

- *I remember how I felt before the exercise session. I feel much better now. Not only do I feel more relaxed, I also feel very good about my accomplishment.*

Thoughts Hours After Exercise

One strategy to help increase your motivation for exercising the next day is called echoing. "Echoing" defines the process of making sure that a pleasant event has a recurring presence during the day. Particularly during periods where you might otherwise be daydreaming about problems, take a moment to reflect on (echo) your exercise success. Thoughts may include the following:

- *I did it; I got in exercise today to help my mood and body.*

- *I can still feel fatigue; I gave myself a good run today.*

- *This feeling in my legs means I am taking care of myself and using my body to help my mood.*

- *I was bothered by the feelings I had during exercise, but I really did it, I am getting stronger.*

- *I have gotten in three exercise sessions so far this week; I am really doing it—I am investing in my own future of a better mood and good health.*

- *Now that I've done several exercise sessions, I can tell that I love the feeling afterwards. It is great to see that such a small investment of time can have such a nice payoff.*

By attending to your periods of success, tracking them, and putting effort into repeating them, you will be helping create motivation for a lifelong health habit. Also, consider echoing all of the useful things you do as a way of life.

Hating Some Exercise Sessions

We want you to know for sure that you will HATE some of your exercise sessions. For example, some runs, for no reason that you can identify, will be lousy. On each step, your legs will feel like they are made of lead. You will feel like you have no energy. You will be paying attention to every breath. And all of the earlier advice on redirecting your attention to more pleasant things will fail. You will hate the run. This happens! But you will still get the benefits of exercise. And your next run may be terrific.

It is important to know that there is nothing about a few miserable exercise sessions that can defeat your ultimate success at becoming a regular exerciser. Expect some bad days, but still finish the exercise each session. You may walk instead of run, take extra breaks, scowl, and swear, but you can bounce back from these episodes. Tell yourself, "It happens; that was no fun, but I still treated my body well and will still get the benefits of whatever exercise I did." Then, expect that tomorrow's exercise session will be better.

Chapter 5   *Initiating Your Exercise Program*

Goals

- To determine if you are medically ready for an exercise program

- To find the right exercise activity for you

- To work toward the recommended dose of exercise

- To learn how to pace your exercise session

- To decide when to exercise

- To address possible barriers to exercise

- To use an exercise log to track your progress

Determining Readiness for an Exercise Program

Before starting your exercise program, we recommend that you work with your clinician to determine whether you need medical clearance. As an initial step, you should complete the AHA/ACSM Health/Fitness Facility Pre-participation Screening Questionnaire provided in this chapter. Be sure to discuss the results and possible indicated follow-up steps with your clinician.

Physical Activity Readiness Questionnaire (PAR-Q)

If you are between the ages of 15 and 69, the PAR-Q will tell you if you should check with your doctor before engaging in physical activity. Common sense is your best guide when you answer these questions. Please read them carefully and answer each one honestly by checking Yes or No.

Yes   No

☐   ☐   1. Has your doctor ever said that you have a heart condition and that you should only do physical activity recommended by a doctor?

☐   ☐   2. Do you feel pain in your chest when you do physical activity?

☐   ☐   3. In the past month, have you had chest pain when you were not doing physical activity?

☐   ☐   4. Do you lose your balance because of dizziness or do you ever lose consciousness?

☐   ☐   5. Do you have a bone or joint problem (e.g., back, knee, or hip) that could be made worse by a change in your physical activity?

☐   ☐   6. Is your doctor currently prescribing drugs (e.g., water pills) for high blood pressure or heart condition?

☐   ☐   7. Do you know of any other reason why you should not engage in physical activity?

If you answered Yes to one or more questions, talk to your doctor **before** beginning a physical activity program.

If you answered No to all questions, you can be reasonably sure that you can start becoming more physically active.

One of the first choices in planning exercise is deciding what might be the most reasonable activity. Walking or running is a popular choice because these activities are readily available. Nonetheless, you and your clinician should consider other available alternatives. The worksheet provided lists some examples of moderate-intensity and vigorous-intensity activities. If you are interested in a more extensive list of activities with corresponding intensity, one is provided online at http://prevention.sph.sc.edu/tools/docs/documents_compendium.pdf. Note that the intensity of each activity listed in this document is expressed in METs (metabolic equivalency tasks). Activities associated with greater than 6 METs are vigorous in intensity; activities of 3–5.9 METs are moderate in intensity.

Selecting Activities Worksheet

Check off or write in the activities that seem most fitting for your exercise interests.

Moderate-intensity exercise

☐ Walking at 3–4 mph

☐ Bicycling on flat ground at 10–12 mph

☐ Swimming leisurely

☐ Doubles tennis

☐ Shooting baskets

☐ _____

☐ _____

☐ _____

Vigorous-intensity exercise

☐ Jogging or running at >4.5 mph

☐ Bicycling on flat ground at >12 mph

☐ Swimming—moderate/hard

☐ Cross-country skiing >2.5 mph

☐ Rollerblading

☐ _____

☐ _____

☐ _____

Research to date is clear in showing mood benefits for exercise. And it appears that these benefits are better when you get a full dose of exercise. The best information on a full dose is provided by the Department of Health and Human Services. According to these guidelines, a full dose of health-giving aerobic exercise is:

1) Moderate-intensity aerobic exercise for at least 150 minutes (2 hours and 30 minutes) each week

OR

2) Vigorous-intensity aerobic exercise for at least 75 minutes (1 hour and 15 minutes) each week.

Moderate-intensity aerobic exercise involves activities that *noticeably* increase your heart rate (e.g., brisk walking), whereas vigorous-intensity activity *substantially* increases your heart rate and causes you to breathe much faster (e.g., jogging). For reducing depression or anxiety, the literature indicates that aerobic exercise should be performed in bouts of at least 25 minutes on 3–5 days a week.

Determining Target Heart Rate

Perhaps the easiest method to determine the intensity of exercise is to simply measure your heart rate during the activity. The target heart rate that corresponds with moderate-intensity exercise is between 64% and 76% of the age-adjusted maximal heart rate (HR_{max}; $220 - age$). Exercise intensity becomes vigorous when your heart rate ranges between 77% and 93% of your HR_{max}. Use the formulas provided to determine your target heart rate.

Determining Target Heart Rate

Moderate-intensity exercise

64–$76\% \times (220 - \text{your age}) = $ _____-_____/%

Vigorous-intensity exercise

77–$93\% \times (220 - \text{your age}) = $ _____-_____/%

Initial Exercise Schedule

Naturally, you want to choose a starting point that will allow you to stay with your exercise habit. Our belief is that, to establish a strong exercise habit, there is no starting level that is too low. Walking several times a week, just to get in the habit of regular exercise, is a more reasonable alternative than overworking during an initial exercise attempt and being sore and resentful during the remainder of the week. Start small and make your habit strong. Figure 5.1 presents a possible schedule for the initial weeks of your exercise program. As you can see, by gradually changing the intensity, duration, and frequency of your exercise sessions, you may take 3 or 4 weeks to get your activity schedule up to the recommended dose. Of course, you and your clinician can decide to use a different schedule to get you to your correct exercise dose.

Week	Exercise intensity	Exercise duration	Exercise frequency
1	65% of HR_{max}	15 min	2 times per week
2	65–70% of HR_{max}	15–20 min	2–3 times per week
3	70–75% of HR_{max}	20–25 min	3–4 times per week
4	75–80% of HR_{max}	25–30 min	3–5 times per week

Figure 5.1

Sample Initial Exercise Training Progression

Determining Initial Exercise Training Progression

Week	Exercise intensity	Exercise duration	Exercise frequency

Pacing Your Exercise Session

In order to maximize your success with exercise and reduce the risk of injury, you should start your exercise session with a warm-up and finish it with a cool-down period. The warm-up period should last between 10 and 15 minutes and should begin with some low-intensity exercise (e.g., slow walking) followed by stretching activities. You should then slowly increase the intensity of your activity until it reaches the lower end of the target heart rate range for that session. Although it is often tempting to stop immediately after you have completed your scheduled activity, we recommend that you allow your body to gradually recover from the intense activity. Finish your routine by walking slowly for approximately 5 minutes and another 5 minutes of stretching.

When to Exercise

Chapter 3 provided you with information on challenges and benefits that are associated with exercise at certain times of the day. Be sure to consider some of these challenges in relation to your personal schedule in deciding when to exercise. To start this process, it is useful to have a clear notion of what your week is like and the natural periods where you are more or less busy or stressed. You may want to choose the higher-stress periods for exercise breaks, but we also understand that it is harder to fit in the time for exercise on those days. Use the Daily Schedule Planner form to write out your schedule of regularly occurring events at the present time, and then work with your clinician to pick times when exercise might best fit into your schedule.

Daily Schedule Planner

	Morning	Mid-Day	Afternoon	Evening
Monday				
Tuesday				
Wednesday				
Thursday				
Friday				
Saturday				
Sunday				

As discussed in Chapters 3 and 4, motivating yourself to exercise may be particularly difficult at the beginning of an exercise-training program, when you haven't experienced any of the benefits. You may find that you don't have the time or it is inconvenient to exercise. You may also find exercise boring or have little confidence in your ability to be active or even have concerns of injury. These barriers to exercise are common. Being aware of your perceived barriers and developing strategies to overcome them may help you be successful in making exercise part of your daily life. Try to take a proactive approach in the planning of your weekly exercise program. As a first step, you may consider writing down your exercise schedule for the week and list possible or anticipated barriers to completing this schedule (see the Exercise Planning Worksheet provided). Then, create a list of possible strategies that you can use to overcome each barrier. It may be useful to enlist the help of your clinician or a friend in this process. They can help you be fair in assessing what stands in the way for you to become more active and can possibly offer some creative solutions to these barriers. Figure 5.2 shows a completed example of the Exercise Planning Worksheet.

My exercise schedule for this week is as follows:			
Monday Activity: _Run_ Intensity: _65% HR max_ Duration: _25 min_	**Tuesday** Activity: _____ Intensity: _____ Duration: _____	**Wednesday** Activity: _Run_ Intensity: _70% HR max_ Duration: _30 min_	**Thursday** Activity: _____ Intensity: _____ Duration: _____
Friday Activity: _____ Intensity: _____ Duration: _____	**Saturday** Activity: _Run_ Intensity: _75% HR max_ Duration: _40 min_	**Sunday** Activity: _____ Intensity: _____ Duration: _____	**SUMMARY** **Intensity:** _65–75%_ **Duration:** _25–40 min_ **Frequency:** _3_
Anticipated barriers		*Possible solutions*	
1. Travel for work		1. Stay at a hotel that has exercise facilities	
		2. Join a gym that has multiple locations in multiple cities	
		3. Join the YMCA or YWCA	
2. Lack of energy		1. Plan to exercise in the morning when I feel most energetic	
		2. Remind myself that my energy increases with exercise	
		3.	

Figure 5.2

Example of Completed Exercise Planning Worksheet

Exercise Planning Worksheet

My exercise schedule for this week is as follows:

Monday	**Tuesday**	**Wednesday**	**Thursday**
Activity: _____	Activity: _____	Activity: _____	Activity: _____
Intensity: _____	Intensity: _____	Intensity: _____	Intensity: _____
Duration: _____	Duration: _____	Duration: _____	Duration: _____
Friday	**Saturday**	**Sunday**	**SUMMARY**
Activity: _____	Activity: _____	Activity: _____	**Intensity:** _____
Intensity: _____	Intensity: _____	Intensity: _____	**Duration:** _____
Duration: _____	Duration: _____	Duration: _____	**Frequency:** _____

Anticipated barriers	*Possible solutions*
1.	1.
	2.
	3.
2.	1.
	2.
	3.

Use of Exercise Logs

The use of exercise logs can be helpful to keep your efforts, strategies, and achievements clear to you. In the beginning of your exercise program, these logs will be fairly detailed and have space for you to record not only your exercise but the impact of exercise on your mood. Completion of these logs after each exercise session should help you track your progress and see the mood benefits of your program. Use a new log for each week of the first 6 weeks of your exercise (or however long it takes you to get up to the recommended public health dose). Additional copies of this form are provided in the appendix.

Exercise for Mood Log

This log is to help me keep track of my exercise goals for mood by focusing on the importance of exercise several days a week.

Week Number _____

	Day 1 Date: __/__	Day 2 Date: __/__	Day 3 Date: __/__	Day 4 Date: __/__	Day 5 Date: __/__	Day 6 Date: __/__	Day 7 Date: __/__
Day of the week							
Exercise completed (✓)							
Time of day of exercise							
Type of exercise completed							
Intensity (%HR$_{max}$)							
Duration (minutes)							
Pre-exercise Feelings/Mood							
Post-exercise Feelings/Mood							

Chapter 6   *Maintaining Your Exercise Program*

Goals

- To fine-tune your exercise program

- To enjoy your exercise treatment gains

- To learn how to bounce back from missed sessions

Fine-tuning Your Exercise Program

Once you have worked up to the minimum recommended public health dose of exercise, your task becomes finding ways to continue to exercise. The aim is for exercise to become a stronger habit and a regular part of your ongoing routine. Following the first weeks of training, it will be useful to consider things you can do to make exercise an easier and better part of your routine. Do there need to be any changes in the timing of your exercise? Now that you are not so new to the program, are there other people you may want to involve in your exercise habit? At this point, it is beneficial to review Chapters 1, 3, and 4 of this workbook to see if there are additional supports you want to put in place for your exercise routine.

Adaptations for Individual Needs

It is also an excellent time to make sure you are adapting your exercise program to your individual needs. Chapter 8 provides additional information on the use of exercise as part of treatment of depression. Chapter 9 extends this information to apply to bipolar disorder and provides additional ideas for working with your clinical team. Chapter 10 is important to review if you are exercising as part of a program to manage anxiety or panic. These chapters offer ideas on how to change or add to your exercise routine to get additional cognitive or mood benefits.

Varying Intensity, Duration, and Frequency

Also, continue to plan how you may want to change your exercise prescription by varying one or more of the following three exercise parameters:

1. Intensity (the target heart rate)

2. Duration (minutes per session)

3. Frequency (number of sessions per week)

You or your clinician may want to make changes in these parameters to help you better achieve your mood and fitness goals. If so, write down your exercise prescription in the space provided.

For management of mood and anxiety disorders in general, the public health dose of exercise should meet your needs. The exception to this general rule is that, for the treatment of panic disorder, you want to make sure you exercise at a sufficient intensity to create the somatic symptoms of exertion (see Figure 10.4 in Chapter 10). Completing at least a 25-minute bout of exercise of this intensity three times a week will help you achieve a healthy dose of exercise while also making sure you become comfortable with stronger sensations of exertion—a goal discussed in detail in Chapter 10. Use your time with your clinician to discuss your thoughts about and experiences with exercise and the changes you note relative to mood or anxiety symptoms.

Your Exercise Prescription

Week	Exercise intensity	Exercise duration	Exercise frequency

Expanding your workout parameters can also add more fun to your exercise routines. As you establish a physical activity habit, you will likely make changes to the specific weekly program. You may want to add new exercises or plan for hard versus easy exercise sessions to create diversity in your routine. Making sure that you have diversity in your exercise experiences will help keep your exercise program interesting. Chapter 11 provides much greater detail on the topic of keeping exercise fresh and enjoyable.

Enjoying Your Exercise Treatment Gains

It is important that you keep attention on the benefits you are attaining with exercise. During and after any given exercise session, make sure you reflect on the gains you are receiving. What are the ways in which you feel better? Do you notice changes in the way you react to stress? Do others in your life notice differences in your mood or the quality of interactions with you? Do you find you have more energy or sleep better due to exercise? Has your sense of the seasons or your town or city changed because exercise gets you outside? Have you developed new friendships because of exercise? Noticing and enjoying these changes will help you settle into your exercise routine and acknowledge your achievements. Don't forget to congratulate yourself for whatever fitness level you have achieved so far in this program.

Bouncing Back From Missed Sessions

It is natural to miss sessions of exercise from time to time. Perhaps the most important aspect of establishing a longer-term exercise habit is becoming good at getting yourself right back into an exercise routine after missed sessions. You will need to be especially wary of the bad coaching that can happen after a missed session. This bad coaching (doom saying) takes a simple miss and translates it into a prescription for exercise failure. Such bad coaching includes the following thoughts:

- *I missed my exercise; I knew I could not stay with it.*

- *Regular exercise is just too hard; why bother.*

- *I wrecked my benefits already; there is no point in continuing.*

- *I missed exercise all this week; I might as well just give up.*

Alternative and useful coaching for missed sessions includes the following:

- *It is a challenge to keep a perfect exercise schedule; no reason to beat myself up. I just need to get back on track with even a short exercise session.*

- *Making sure I exercise tomorrow will make it easier to get back to my full routine next week.*

- *I am doing this for my mood; not feeling like exercising is not a reason to miss.*

- *I like feeling in shape, and if I exercise later today, I get to keep and extend this feeling.*

- *I have to remember to exercise first, and expect to feel like exercising only after I am back on track.*

Also, to help yourself return from a lapse, you may want to return to the Exercise for Mood Log or forms in the appendix. Continue to work on barriers to exercise as needed. Make sure you track, notice, and enjoy the mood benefits your next few exercise sessions bring.

Chapter 7

Extending Your Exercise Program—Enjoyable Activities and Sleep

Goals

- To keep a regular activity schedule

- To increase pleasant activities

- To improve sleep quality

Overview

To help you get the most out of this program, this chapter is devoted to discussing activity and sleep interventions for expanding your attainment of well-being from exercise.

Keeping a Regular Activity Schedule

Your exercise program is designed to provide you with a natural and effective mood lift. To make the most of this mood lift, it is important to provide yourself with a balance of activities that are pleasurable and that lead to a sense of accomplishment.

As you did with exercise, you can also use the Daily Schedule Planner to help you to structure a personalized weekly activity pattern that works for you. The first step in adding in additional pleasant events in your life is to think about some of the enjoyable activities that you used to do or want to do. Once you identify these activities, write them in the worksheet provided.

Valued Activities

Social Activities

_____

_____

_____

Relationship Activities

_____

_____

_____

Volunteer Activities

_____

_____

_____

Recreation/Entertainment

_____

_____

_____

Hobbies

_____

_____

_____

Work-Related Activities

_____

_____

_____

As exercise and activity increase as part of your exercise program, your desire for pleasant events may increase as well. Use the Daily Schedule Planner from Chapter 5 to better understand your average weekly schedule and to consider what changes you might like to make. Strive for a balance of regularly scheduled small activities or events to help you feel good. These events can be simple pleasant events (lunch with a friend, time for a hobby, a regular movie night, a special television show, etc.) as well as those activities that give you a sense of achievement (gardening, cleaning off your desk, finishing a project, etc.). As you take time to think about and schedule regular involvement in pleasant activities, consider the list of potentially pleasurable activities shown here. The value of this list is in encouraging you to consider a range of pleasant activities. Engaging in rewarding activities on a regular basis serves as a buffer against stress. Note many of these activities involve physical activity, and hence many of these may be easier or more pleasurable to complete as you become more fit.

Pleasant Events List

The following list is designed to stimulate ideas for activities that may increase your weekly pleasure level as well as provide stress-buffering effects. In considering the list, think of the *variations on themes* that may make an activity especially rewarding. For example, little things added to a regular activity—buying your favorite childhood candy at the movie theater or fixing a cup of tea to drink while reading a novel—can help transform an experience by evoking past pleasant memories.

As you go through the list, check off those activities of most interest to you.

- Go fishing in a local stream or pond
- Call two friends and go bowling
- Play with a Frisbee
- Take a kid to mini golf
- Take a yoga class
- Go to an indoor rock climbing center—take a lesson
- Build a snow fort and have a snowball fight
- Walk in the snow and listen to your footsteps
- Catch snowflakes in your mouth
- Sign up for a sculpting class
- Bake a cake
- Draw
- Paint (oils, acrylics, watercolor)
- Climb a tree
- Go for an evening drive
- Go to a drive-in movie
- See a movie
- Volunteer to work at a soup kitchen
- Join a museum Friday night event
- Write a letter to a friend
- Sing a song

- Read the newspaper in a coffee shop
- Schedule a kissing-only date with your romantic partner
- Order hot chocolate in a restaurant
- Buy flowers for the house
- Get a massage
- Reread a book you read in high school or college
- Bake cookies for a neighbor
- Have a garage sale (perhaps with a neighbor)
- Buy a spool of wire, and make a sculpture
- Go to an art museum and find one piece you really like
- Buy a magazine on a topic you know nothing about
- Polish all of your shoes
- Buy a new plant
- Clean out a closet
- Write a letter to the editor of the local newspaper
- Repaint a table or a shelf

continued

- Play a musical instrument
- Take an art class
- Walk a dog
- Volunteer to walk dogs for a local animal shelter
- Play with children
- Visit a pet shop and look at the animals
- Sit in the sun
- Sit on a porch swing
- Go for a hike
- Learn to knit
- Do a crossword puzzle (each day for a week)
- Go out for an ice cream sundae
- Rent a garden plot at a local farm or community space
- Grill dinner in the back yard
- Take a bath at night with candles around the tub
- Have a picnic at a park with a friend
- Have a tea party on your or your neighbor's front porch
- Go bird/nature watching
- Read a book under a tree
- Organize photos/CD collection
- Write poetry
- Join a choir or singing group
- Do Sudoku puzzles
- Put on some dance music and dance in your living room
- Sign up for a class at the local community college or center
- Go to a diner for breakfast
- Devote a meal to cooking red, white, and blue foods
- Plan an affordable 3-day vacation
- Start a collection of heart-shaped rocks
- Find your top three favorite videos on YouTube and share them with a friend
- Woodworking—build a table or a chair
- Burn a CD of your favorite movie music
- Take a dance class
- Learn to fold dollar bills into origami creatures
- Soak your feet in warm water
- Learn to juggle
- Clean and polish the inside of your car
- Go to a concert
- Meditate
- Organize a weekly game of cribbage or bridge
- Look at a map
- Plan a drive in the country
- Sew some napkins
- Make a pizza and bake it
- Buy a cookbook and make three new meals
- Read a novel
- Listen to your favorite song from high school . . . really loudly

continued

- Make a scrapbook
- Read travel books about places you've always wanted to visit (and maybe plan a visit!)
- Play charades
- Go to the beach
- Go to the zoo
- Start writing a journal
- Play pub trivia
- Learn a new language
- Take a photo every day for a week
- Have a poker night
- Play horseshoes
- Go to a sporting event
- Play ping-pong
- Invite friends over for board games

- Rent a video, make popcorn, and invite friends over
- Attend a local art event (a dance performance, a play, an art show opening)
- Go to a comedy club
- Join a book club
- Join an after-school program to mentor children
- Lie by a pool/river/lake/beach
- Take a historic tour of your city
- Get dressed up and go for dinner with your romantic partner or friends
- Have a neighborhood barbeque
- Play video games

Sleep Quality

As you start and work to maintain your program of exercise, it is helpful to also get the most out of your sleep time. Exercise will naturally help you feel nicely fatigued (physical fatigue feels different than mental fatigue) and ready to sleep. To complement this process, it is important to make sure you don't have any bad sleep habits that may be reducing the quality of your sleep time. The following tips will—in general—maximize the quality of your sleep.

Good Sleep Strategies

- Eliminate stress in the bedroom. Discussions about your life or family issues or evening work (e.g., paying bills and reading documents for work) should not take place in bed or in the bedroom. Save the bedroom for bed activities. Worry or work at a desk, not in bed.

- Give yourself time to unwind before sleep. Make sure the last hour of activity before bedtime is relatively passive. Do not pay bills, do not work out life problems, and do not plan your workday just before going to bed; save these activities for earlier in the day when you are fresher. Before sleep, choose activities that are pleasant and take very little effort (e.g., television, reading, and talking). Go to bed only after you have had a chance to unwind and feel more like sleeping.

- Use a regular daytime cycle to help with nighttime sleep. Avoid taking naps during the day. Use regular exercise (at least 3 hours before bedtime) to help increase sleep and induce normal fatigue. One way to establish a regular time for falling asleep is to have a regular time for waking up. Setting your alarm clock to a reasonable time and maintaining it throughout the week will eventually be helpful in stabilizing your sleep time.

- Reduce caffeine use (certainly eliminate caffeine use after noon), and be wary of drinking alcohol or smoking within several hours of bedtime.

- If you have sleep problems, be careful of trying too hard to get to sleep. Trying hard to get to sleep often has the opposite effect; it wakes a person up with feelings of frustration and anger. Instead, try to enjoy being in bed and resting, even if sleep does not come. Direct your attention to how comfortable you are in bed (how the pillow feels or how good it feels to lie down and stretch), how relaxed your muscles feel, and how you can let your thoughts drift. If sleep does not come in a reasonable time, get out of bed and do a calm activity in another room. Return to bed only when you feel sleepy.

- Use muscle relaxation techniques in bed. Relaxation tapes may help you relax and feel even more comfortable in bed. Remember the goal is not to go to sleep but to become very comfortable in bed so that sleep comes naturally. Commercially available relaxation tapes may help with this process.

Chapter 8   *Exercise Targeted to Depression*

Goals

- To learn about the thinking patterns that accompany depression

- To take advantage of the beneficial effects of exercise

- To use self-coaching

- To use your support team

- To sustain and increase your activity level

Model of Depression

Depression is much more than the sad or blue mood people sometimes experience when they have had a bad day. Major depression is a medical disorder that is characterized by a constellation of symptoms that are present daily or nearly every day for a minimum of two weeks. Symptoms of depression include those listed in the Symptoms to Be Targeted by Exercise form in Chapter 1: blue mood, lack of interest, feelings of guilt, low energy, disrupted appetite, agitation or difficulties moving, sleep disruptions, and, at times, suicidal thoughts. Some or all of these symptoms may be present during depression, and their severity can make it difficult to function in life.

Negative Thinking

Depression, like many psychiatric disorders, involves a number of self-perpetuating cycles. The low mood leads to more negative thinking patterns and expectations of failure and disappointment. For example, when depressed, it is common for people to have negative thoughts about the following:

- oneself ("I blew it"; "I am no good"; "It never works out for me"; "Look at me, I am . . .", etc.)

- others ("He does not care about me"; "They don't like me"; etc.)

- the future ("It won't work out"; "There is no point"; etc.)

- ongoing goals, including one's exercise program ("Exercise is doing nothing for me"; "There is no point in continuing")

This type of thinking can worsen a depressed mood, increase feelings of hopelessness, and decrease engagement in useful behaviors and problem solving. Not only will you have thoughts of this kind, but these thoughts will also *feel* more true during periods of stress and depression. Moreover, it is important to remember that *negative thoughts do not have to be true to have a powerful effect on your emotions.* It is important that you treat your thoughts as rough guesses about the world rather than as true statements of what is going on. And these guesses have as much to do with your current mood state and thinking habits as they do about external reality.

Repetitive Thoughts

Another feature of thinking patterns in depression is the focus on repetitive thoughts. Depressed individuals may find that they turn the same thought over and over again (ruminations) with no useful outcome. When cognitively ruminating, you never get a break from your problems, and have little ability to notice that better, less painful things may be going on in your life. Thinking this way can be like putting your tongue in the socket of a missing tooth: It hurts, but at the same time, it feels almost irresistible to check and see if it still hurts! Because of this, ruminations can be a strong force in keeping your mood low.

Beneficial Effects of Exercise

One useful aspect of hard aerobic exercise is that it is very hard to keep ruminating during and after the exercise. In fact, one of the early effects you may notice that exercise such as running has on depression is that, during the last half of your exercise period, you may notice that your mind becomes quiet. Instead of having ongoing ruminations, you may begin to notice other feelings and events—the sky, the trees, your music. With ongoing running, your mind may return to how you are when not depressed.

This program wants you to be prepared to take advantage of this effect. When exercising to help relieve depression, be prepared to have a rumination-free period during your exercise session. Prior to running, for example, you may want to instruct yourself, "This run is a time when I *do not* have to think about how I feel or focus on my negative thoughts. This will be an opportunity to just be in the moment, feeling whatever I feel during the run, and enjoying my music and the sights along my running route."

Coaching

Also, when exercising to relieve depression, it will be important for you to put in extra effort to coach yourself effectively. Because of depression, you may have a number of negative and motivation-sapping thoughts:

- *Why bother, nothing is going to help this depression.*

- *Who cares! I feel so bad already; exercise will just make me feel worse.*

- *I just want to be in bed; I will run tomorrow.*

When you have these kinds of thoughts, the goal is to be effective at *listening to the chatter but exercising anyway.*

It is not helpful to get into a cycle of trying too hard to change your thoughts. Instead, focus on the role of thoughts—they are to be useful to you, and if they are not useful, then don't let them direct your behavior. In depression, your thoughts will naturally become overnegative, and you will have to be very careful about placing too much credence in them. When depressed, you may want to practice treating some of your negative thoughts like they are wayward children. You understand why the thoughts want to go wandering off in the direction in which they go, but you don't need to follow them. For example, when faced by the negative thoughts about running, you may want to say the following to yourself:

Yes, it is possible that . . .

- *Exercise won't work for me*

- *I should just stay in bed*

- *Lying down or watching television now would be comforting*

But, now is my scheduled exercise time. I will see what I feel like doing after I exercise.

Using Your Support Team

When exercising to help treat your depression, you will want to use every available situational support. Ask one of your support team members (identified in Chapter 1) to encourage you to exercise. Be specific in telling this person how you want coaching. "Please give me a call weekly and ask me how my exercise program is going; I like the idea of having someone to talk to about it." Or, "I would love it if you could walk with me weekly. I am trying to keep up with a new exercise program. Knowing that we could walk together would really help me stay with it, and you will get the benefits as well."

Sustaining and Increasing Activity Levels

One effect of depression is a reduced activity level. And with reduced activity, individuals with depression are cut off from the very activities that could help restore their mood. In addition to the direct lifts in mood that can come after a session of exercise, merely sustaining your activity levels (by exercising several times a week) can help extend exercise's antidepressant effects.

To achieve a balanced lifestyle, exercise should be one part of a series of mood-enhancing activities. Recommendations for this goal are provided in Chapter 7. After you have established a regular exercise habit, add in other pleasurable events that help promote a positive mood. Use the list of pleasant events in Chapter 7 as well as the Daily Schedule Planner to schedule these "buffering" events. We call them buffering events because they can help buffer the effects of a low mood or a stressful week. Having something to look forward to, even if you feel blue, and participating in these activities can have powerful effects on reducing depression.

Chapter 9

Bipolar Disorder and Exercise

Goals

- To learn about bipolar disorder and its treatment

- To use exercise as an adjunct to treatment for bipolar disorder

- To challenge loaded words and phrases

About Bipolar Disorder and Its Treatment

Bipolar disorder is a relatively common psychiatric disorder that in its classic form affects 1–2% of the population. Bipolar disorder is characterized by recurrent episodes of mood disturbance that occurs on two poles: periods of depression and periods of mood elevation, where individuals feel so hyper that they feel they are not their normal selves. These periods of elevated mood meet criteria for mania when the moods are accompanied by symptoms such as racing thoughts, inflated self-esteem, decreased need for sleep, and over-participation in activities (gambling, risky sex, extramarital affairs, investments, etc.) that have a high potential for harm. There are a number of subtypes of bipolar disorder that are defined by the degree of elevated mood (full mania or an attenuated version of mania called "hypomania"). Likewise individuals may differ whether their bipolar disorder is characterized by the down periods—the depressions that define the other pole of bipolar disorder. In most cases, it is more common to find individuals suffering from the depressive symptoms than manic symptoms in bipolar disorder. However, because of the cyclic nature of the disorder, treatment efforts in bipolar disorder are aimed at elimination of the current mood episodes as well as prevention of the next episode.

Treatment for Bipolar Disorder

For decades, the dominant treatment for bipolar disorder was an exclusive focus on medications and the application of a variety of mood stabilizing, antipsychotic, antidepressant, and anti-anxiety medications to the management of the disorder. Recently, however, a variety of studies have documented that certain types of psychotherapy can have powerful effects for treating bipolar disorder as well as helping prevent relapse. Certain types of psychotherapies for depression, such as cognitive-behavioral therapy, have been applied more or less directly to bipolar depression with promising results. These findings give us some confidence that exercise interventions, shown to be effective for treating depression, will have similar effects on bipolar depression.

There are a number of additional reasons to expect that exercise may be important for the broader management of bipolar disorder. First, there is evidence that programmed exercise can reduce stress and anxiety among patients with bipolar disorder, and both stress and anxiety have been implicated in both the higher number and greater severity of mood episodes. Second, stability of sleep–wake patterns have been shown important in the management of bipolar disorder, and exercise offers benefits for sleep quality and stability. Third, interventions for bipolar frequently include programs to structure sleep, wake, and activity cycles more generally, and exercise can be play an important role in this overall moderation of emotional arousal and activity. Fourth, periods of irritability and anger characterize many bipolar patterns, and large-scale studies have shown less anger and cynical distrust among individuals who exercise frequently. Accordingly, for an individual with bipolar disorder, exercise may help calm feelings of irritability and anger that can emerge as part of both poles (depression as well as mania) of bipolar patterns. Finally, some of the medications used to help manage mood variability in bipolar disorder can lead to significant weight gain. In response to this challenge, a number of specialty clinics for bipolar disorder are beginning to consider lifestyle management programs that offer exercise as a weight control strategy for patients needing to take these medications. Hence, exercise, in addition to providing direct effects for mood management, can also provide some benefit for reducing some of the side effects (weight gain) of other treatments for bipolar disorder.

Using Exercise in Bipolar Disorder

In considering bipolar disorder, it is important to underscore the fact that mood-stabilizing medications continue to be the core treatment for bipolar disorder, and exercise should be considered as an adjunct and not as a replacement for this treatment. Exercise provides an additional and active element of treatment that patients can own and can apply on a near daily basis. For this reason, exercise is sometimes an especially pleasing option for individuals with bipolar disorder because it does involve such active and personal effort as compared to medication use alone. Indeed, bipolar disorder is one of those conditions where a full application of medication treatment, psychotherapy, and exercise may provide patients with a crucially broad basis for managing mood symptoms.

An additional element of an exercise program for application to bipolar disorder is the focus on balance. Exercise is to be applied as a regular part of a near daily routine. It is to be applied regardless of individual ups and down in mood, and individuals with bipolar disorder should view it as the time of the day to lock in moderation. The goal is for exercise to work like clockwork in your schedule, providing a break that can be relied upon.

Also, you can use your monitoring of your exercise as an index of your mood. Moderation is the key, and you will need to monitor urges to over-exercise or skip exercise. These urges may be part of a normal pattern of wanting a break from a routine, but with bipolar disorder it pays to also ask the question: "Is this part of my normal variability in interest, or is this a sign that I should watch whether this is a symptom of a mood episode?" In either case, early intervention (calling your clinician and discussing options) is especially important for the overall management of bipolar disorder. In addition to a program of exercise, we strongly recommend attending to creating a balanced and rewarding activity schedule as discussed in Chapter 7.

Loaded Words and Phrases

The previous chapter gave recommendations to *notice* your thoughts, *observe* how the thoughts make you feel, and to gently *redirect* your thoughts. For the management of bipolar disorder, you will also want to be adept in noticing the form your thoughts take, with particular attention to the presence of "loaded words." Loaded words are words or phrases that evoke lots of emotion despite being inaccurate. They are exaggerations of everyday outcomes, and they have the effect of making us feel worse than we need to feel. With loaded words, minor social mishaps become "disasters," a less than optimal outcome becomes a "failure," and mistakes become evidence that we are "so stupid." The consequence of these thoughts is that everyday events feel more dire and depressing. Also, when you are feeling more down, you will tend to use thoughts like these when thinking about yourself.

This program wants to sensitize you to these thoughts so that when you hear them, you can redirect yourself toward more accurate thinking. You can do this by challenging your assessment ("What do I really mean by 'disaster'? What about this situation really deserves that label?"). The goal is to help you react realistically to situations rather than reacting to overly emotional descriptions of the situation. Use the Replacing Loaded Words and Phrases worksheet as needed.

Replacing Loaded Words and Phrases

Appraisal with loaded words	Accurate appraisal and planning
It was a _____ ▪ Disaster ▪ Nightmare ▪ Terrible ▪ _____	I don't think the event went well because of (be specific) _____ _____ _____
I was a _____ ▪ Failure ▪ Loser ▪ Reject ▪ _____	Next time it would be better if I (be specific) _____ _____ _____ _____

Chapter 10   *Stress, Worry, and Panic Disorder*

Goals

- To recognize and defer worries

- To learn about panic attacks and panic disorder

- To learn about the treatment for panic disorder

- To apply exercise to panic disorder

Introduction

We have all had those moments when we just can't get worried thoughts out of our head. They come in over and over again. Worry is a self-perpetuating process. Worries about problems increase feelings of stress and anxiety, and these feelings make our worries and anxiety-provoking thoughts *feel* more true.

When stress and anxiety is strong—when we feel a tight chest, sweaty palms, queasy stomach, racing heart, and dizziness—anxious thoughts can be particularly hard to dismiss. We can lose control of the process of useful problem solving. We lose perspective! And we may even know that we have lost perspective and that a mental breather would be useful. But the thoughts may have taken on a life of their own, and it is hard to turn away from anxious ruminations. Exercise may be just the perfect action to take in these moments. Exercise can help you reset your mood and thoughts and provide you with several hours of calmer and clearer thinking after you exercise. The key is remembering to use exercise at these moments.

Recognizing and Deferring Worries

Anxiety-inducing thoughts are often in the form of "what if . . ." (What if I get fired? What if he breaks up with me? What if the kids get sick? What if she is mad? What if the report is flawed? What if things get worse?). In anxiety conditions

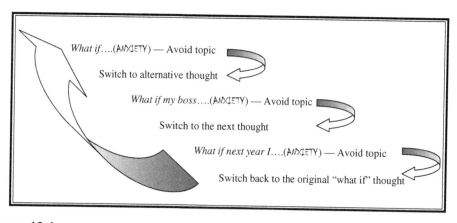

Figure 10.1

Diagram of the Worry Process

typified by worry, it is common for individuals to bring up an anxiety-provoking thought, experience the emotional cost of the thought (increased anxiety and tension), and then shift to an alternative thought. If we would diagram the process, it would look something like Figure 10.1.

In many cases, individuals under stress just need a break so that they can regain perspective rather than being caught in a cycle of unproductive-anxious thinking. An exercise session can be just the thing to give you a break from these thoughts and—most importantly—give you perspective. You can then engage in productive problem solving (actually thinking about solutions rather than ruminating about potential problems).

However, it is unlikely you will be at a point in the day when you can take an exercise break when you are in the middle of stress or anxiety. Instead, you will need to practice *deferring* worry and rumination until you can get perspective. When you feel yourself in a loop of anxious thoughts, we want you to ask yourself, "Do I really need to think about this now, and is my thinking leading to solutions?" You may want to coach yourself by saying something like the following:

> "I don't need to think about this all the time. It feels good to have a break from these thoughts. What can I notice in the *here and now* that is more pleasant than turning over 'what if' thoughts in my mind?"

Then, during your next exercise session, allow yourself to use your exercise and physical exertion to provide you with a period of perspective. Your goal is to use the natural effects of exercise to induce a worry-free period and to create a sense of calmness to help you stay worry-free for hours after exercise.

Panic Attacks and Panic Disorder

At times, anxiety comes on so suddenly and so strongly that it becomes frightening in its own right. These episodes of extreme anxiety are marked by physical symptoms such as dizziness, numbness, tingling, breathlessness, heart palpitations, sweating, and unreality. They are called panic attacks, and panic disorder is an anxiety condition characterized by recurrent panic attacks. Each of the symptoms of a panic attack makes sense. The physical symptoms are either a direct effect of anxiety (e.g., rapid heart rate, rapid breathing, sweating) or a secondary effect of other symptomatic responses (e.g., rapid breathing can rapidly lead to feelings of dizziness and unreality). These symptoms are commonplace at times of fear and are a natural reaction to danger. In an actual dangerous situation (for example, being threatened by another person), attention is focused on the actual threat rather than these symptoms. However, if these anxiety symptoms occur out of the blue, they can become a focus of attention in their own right.

In panic disorder, it is not uncommon for individuals to interpret these symptoms as a sign of one or more of the following:

- impending death ("Am I having a heart attack?"; "Am I having a stroke?"; "I am going to die")

- impending loss of control ("I will faint"; "I am going to have to run out of the room"; "I can't find my way out or take care of the kids")

- impending humiliation ("They are going to notice my symptoms and I will be humiliated"; "They will think I am crazy"; "They will think I am a fool").

These interpretations are of course among the most frightening thoughts a person can have. If believed, these thoughts should motivate the very anxiety reactions that are feared. This is the essence of panic disorder. It is a disorder characterized by the fear of anxiety sensations—the fear of fear itself!

Panic disorder, with or without the avoidance of feared situations (agoraphobia), occurs in about 3% of adults. Panic attacks themselves are much more common, but the full disorder is diagnosed only when the panic attacks are a source of concern themselves. In the full disorder, panic attacks on the order of several times a week are common. Individuals with panic disorder become so concerned about the possibility of having these attacks, avoidance of a wide variety of situations where these attacks might occur (agoraphobia) is common. Avoided situations frequently include those where escape may be difficult (should a panic attack occur)—for example, buses, bridges, long lines, crowded rooms, subways, driving far from home, movie theatres, and shopping malls.

Panic disorder frequently has onset after a period of stress, but what appears to put people at risk for the disorder are tendencies to fear anxiety-related sensations. In addition, once panic disorder develops, it both sensitizes people toward and intensifies this fear of symptoms. Fears of symptoms take the usual "what if" form that characterizes other anxiety-provoking thoughts:

- *What if other people notice?*

- *What if I have a heart attack?*

- *What if I fall down?*

- *What if it gets worse, I lose control and I start to scream?*

- *What if I go crazy?*

- *What if I have a stroke?*

After initial attacks, a self-perpetuating pattern can develop to maintain and worsen the panic attacks. Vigilance to anxiety sensations ("I hope it does not happen now; is my heart beating fast yet?"), memories of past attacks ("last time was horrible, I hope that does not happen again"), and fears of future attacks ("I am starting to lose control; it could be worse than ever") all combine to amplify initial signs of anxiety into a full panic attack. With repeated panic attacks, the body may directly start to respond to signs of arousal (rapid heart rate, sweating, dizziness, etc.) by firing what we call the alarm reaction.

Over time, individuals with panic disorder can become sensitized to these sensations regardless of their source. For example, coffee and exercise produce only mild sensations similar to anxiety (increased heart rate, sweating, and trembling), but because these sensations are linked to the fears of panic

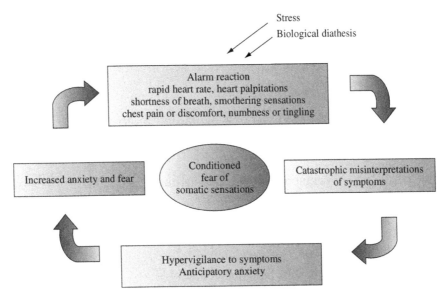

Figure 10.2

Cognitive-Behavioral Model of Panic Disorder

attacks, individuals with panic disorder may avoid them. One result is that individuals with panic disorder always feel on alert for the next attack, vigilant to their symptoms and ready to tense up and try to avoid or control these sensations. This essential pattern underlying panic disorder is summarized in Figure 10.2.

Treatment of Panic Disorder

One of the most effective treatments for panic disorder is cognitive-behavioral therapy. Reviewing your symptoms with your clinician can help confirm whether you have a diagnosis of panic disorder. If you do, you will want to learn about the disorder and its treatment. The core elements of cognitive-behavioral therapy for panic disorder include information about the disorder, help in eliminating the power of "what if" thoughts, and exposure to the feared sensations associated with anxiety and panic. As noted, a variety of these sensations can be induced by vigorous exercise, and as such, exercise can be used as part of treatment for panic disorder.

With vigorous exercise, you can learn to eliminate fears of anxiety sensations by taking charge and becoming comfortable with these natural sensations of autonomic arousal. Vigorous exercise will naturally produce any of a number of odd sensations:

- Rapid heart rate or a "pounding" heart

- Rapid breathing

- A feeling of a heavy chest (from breathing hard)

- Heavy legs

- Sweating

- Dizziness or light-headedness

- Dry mouth or throat

- Numb hands (while running)

The goal is to let yourself become comfortable with these sensations and embrace them as natural and expected. This training can then be transferred back to similar sensations that may arise due to anxiety and panic. Once you learn to undo the fear of these sensations, you can undo the self-perpetuating nature of panic. That is, you can undo the fear-of-fear cycle. The shift from fearing symptoms to becoming comfortable with them is exemplified by Figure 10.3. The goal is to do nothing to control the sensations, but to "relax with" them.

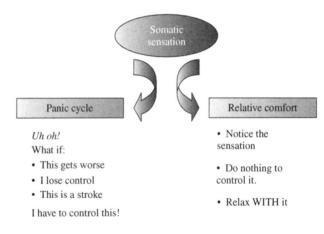

Figure 10.3

Reacting Differently to Panic Sensations

As you increase the intensity of your exercise (as your fitness increases), part of the goal will be to exercise vigorously enough to produce bodily sensations similar to those you experience during a panic attack. Prior to and during this vigorous exercise, you will want to:

1) Remind yourself of what sensations you are going to feel so that there are no surprises (e.g., dizziness, rapid heart rate, light-headedness).

2) Complete the exercise, fully expecting to experience these sensations

3) Notice the sensations and see how comfortable you can get exercising *while having the sensations.*

After you complete the exercise, try not to be waiting for the sensations to go away. Just become good at tolerating them. Remind yourself that it does not matter how long they last because they are not dangerous (your physician has approved your exercise); therefore, you don't have to get rid of these sensations.

Increasing Target Heart Rate

To help treat panic disorder, exercise intensity will have to be high enough to induce the bodily sensations that you experience during a panic attack. For this purpose, you may want to increase the target heart range for your exercise sessions to the middle or high range (80–85% HR_{max}) of vigorous-intensity exercise (see Figure 10.4). Write in your exercise prescription for targeting panic in the space provided.

Your Exercise Prescription for Targeting Panic

Week	Exercise intensity	Exercise duration	Exercise frequency

Week	Exercise Intensity	Exercise Duration	Exercise Frequency
5	75% of HR_{max}	20 minutes	3 times per week
6	80% of HR_{max}	20 minutes	3 times per week
7	85% of HR_{max}	20–25 minutes	3–4 times per week
8	85% of HR_{max}	25–30 minutes	3–5 times per week

Figure 10.4

Example of Completed Exercise Prescription for Targeting Panic

Exercise Practice Log for Panic-Related Concerns

To help you with the task of becoming comfortable with intense bodily sensations, you may want to keep a log of your experiences during vigorous exercise. An Exercise Practice Log for Panic-Related Concerns is provided at the end of this chapter, and additional copies are provided in the appendix at the end of this workbook. The log is designed to draw your attention to the sensations you experienced during exercise and help you become confident that they are safe. You are asked to record the sensations, rate their intensity on a 0 to 100 scale, and rate whether the experience of anxiety was associated with anxiety on the same scale. Then you are asked to examine whether the symptoms had any true adverse consequences for you relative to your fears of these sensations. This information is to be brought for review with your clinician to help you consolidate some of the gains you are achieving from exercise.

Exercise Practice Log for Panic-Related Concerns

Date of Exercise: _____

What sensations did you experience during your exercise?

_____

_____

How intense were the sensations during your workout (0–100)?

Beginning   :

Half-way   :

Toward the end   :

What was your anxiety level throughout the session (0–100)?

Beginning   :

Half-way   :

Toward the end   :

What were the consequences of the sensations that you experienced?

_____

_____

How did these consequences differ from the fears you had of these sensations due to your panic disorder?

_____

_____

What do you want to tell yourself about these sensations now?

_____

_____

_____

Chapter 11

Exercising Over the Long Term

Goals

- To add variety to your exercise routine

- To set new goals

- To make use of other resources (classes, competitions)

- To continue logging your exercise sessions

- To handle lapses in your exercise program

- To make exercise a way of life

Overview

The key to maintaining a strong exercise habit over time is variation. Although you may stay with the exact same exercise over time, the way in which you do it, the features you attend to, and the goals that are meaningful to you are likely to change. This program encourages this process, and this chapter discusses some ways you can add variations to your exercise program to keep it fresh, interesting, and rewarding.

Variation: The Key to Long-Term Success

Many of the changes you may want to consider are subtle. For example, changing the music you listen to, or changing music for radio programs or books on tape, can renew the fun you experience during exercise. For example, if exercise becomes a time to listen to music you enjoy (e.g., to try out a new CD), then it becomes easier to look forward and settle into the exercise time regardless of your interest in "working out." Likewise, changing where you exercise (trying a new gym, changing your running route, inviting along a new exercise partner) can be a powerful way to make sure that exercise time feels like quality time.

In fact, as exercise becomes easier and more automatic, you may well find that you have a greater ability to supplement exercise with other features (attending to music, friends, or the view of your route) to make your exercise time feel much more like personal time. Moreover, if you are meeting the goal of working out four times a week, feel the freedom to make at least one of these weekly exercise episodes particularly special. For example, if you choose walking or running for your exercise, you may want to consider driving to a new location for your exercise (e.g., "it would be fun to run today through that cute town off Route 2").

Setting New Goals

Another important feature of keeping exercise interesting over the longer term is allowing your goals for exercise to change. The primary aim for exercise, relative to this workbook, is to achieve mood benefits. Nonetheless, over time continued exercise will possibly lead to other changes, including weight loss and changes in the shape of your body. Consequently, attending to and enjoying these changes are appropriate strategies for longer-term programs of exercise. However, you will want to make sure that these goals are appropriate to the *timeline* of change. For example, it takes quite a few weeks to change body shape. For this reason, you will not want to make changes in body shape a primary goal—it is just too hard to exercise only for this longer-term outcome. But, if you are exercising because it helps you feel good *now*, then it is also appropriate to enjoy the longer-term changes in body shape. So, don't get in a hurry to achieve results, but do enjoy the body shape changes that occur.

If you are losing weight with exercise, it is because you have changed the basic equation necessary for weight loss—expending more calories than you are taking in. And, it is likely that you have done so in the preferred way—increasing the burning of calories with exercise rather than just restricting your eating. Also, with regular exercise and the mood benefits it brings, you may find yourself less interested in eating as a strategy for coping with feeling down, bored, or lethargic.

A number of body shape changes may be taking place as you exercise, independent of weight change. Certain muscles will be becoming stronger, and as you continue to enjoy exercise, you may choose different body shape goals. For example, you may want to select exercises to reshape the chest and neck, the abdominals, or the hips or thighs. Personal trainers are experts at how to target these regions; otherwise you can consult books and supportive Web sites (see Chapter 3) for help with this process.

Use of Other Resources: Classes and Competition

Once your body begins to respond to exercise and you feel yourself getting in shape, you may want to consider other ways to increase or assess your fitness. Other resources include the use of classes or enjoyable competition events. Classes can extend the range of activities in which you can comfortably participate. They can also lead you a long way forward in developing a group of supportive co-exercisers. For competitive events, the key here is to focus only on those that you find enjoyable. In most cities, there is a wide variety of competitions available. For example, events for running range from charity walks or runs, fun runs (particularly on holidays), community races, to serious competitions. In recent years, access to half marathons, marathons, and triathlons has increased dramatically. For many of the casual participants in these events, the goal is to finish, or finish with a sense of competence, rather than to finish with a certain time in mind. These events are useful for honing training efforts (there is something specific to practice and strive for in weekly exercises). They also provide a sense of group participation, a day of activity and celebration, and often a t-shirt or other reward for participating. The water stations, free water, fruit, or yogurt at the finish stations also add a nice level of drama and reward to the day of the race.

If you think any of these features would be useful to help you gain more joy from your exercise routine, check Web sites and running clubs in your local area for information. Also, it is important to know that competitions can extend to a range of other activities including gym-based competitions, swimming clubs (see Master's clubs on the Web), sport clubs (softball, volleyball, basketball, and hockey), and specialized competitions such as rock climbing.

Logging Exercise

As exercise becomes more of a habit, the log sheets this workbook has provided you thus far will lose some of their usefulness. The Monthly Exercise Log is designed to help you keep a diary of the nature and quality of your exercise program. It offers you a way to target frequent exercise (averaging four days a week) and keep track of trends in your exercise, including exercise sessions you found particularly enjoyable. It also provides you with space for coaching yourself toward new exercise goals. This form is included in this chapter, and additional copies are included in the appendix. If you prefer to log your exercise session online instead of on paper, or are interested in logging other health habits (e.g., sleep or nutrition) as well, you may want to join a free service like MapMyRun (http://www.mapmyrun.com) or FitLink (http://www.fitlink.com).

Monthly Exercise Log

Exercise session	Exercise completed	Duration and intensity	Notes and plans
1			
2			
3			
4			
5			
6			
7			
8			
9			
10			
11			
12			
13			
14			
15			
16			
Bonus			
Bonus			
Bonus			

Comments on the month: _____

Special goals or plans for the next month: _____

Handling Lapses in Your Exercise Program

As you exercise over time, you may also face the reality of lapses in your exercise habit. There may be times that you slip away from regular exercise, suddenly discovering that you have gone for a week or two with no organized activity. If this happens, you will need to be a good coach to yourself with the following steps:

1) Understand that such slips in motivation are natural.

2) Take some time to think what can be done to make your next exercise session especially enjoyable.

3) Remind yourself that you are exercising to feel good.

4) Try to restart your exercise routine before you start to feel a change in your fitness level.

Keep in mind that going back to exercise when you are feeling fit, regardless of your level of motivation in the moment, is a much easier process than waiting for stronger motivation to return. Remember to exercise first, and feel the motivation to exercise second.

Exercise as a Way of Life

As you continue to exercise, you will find yourself developing habits that further support your exercise goals. You may find yourself having a variety of workout clothes, and that you perfected the process of where to hang sweaty clothes as they await time in the washer. You may find yourself looking forward to the feeling of muscle heaviness or soreness that follows a particularly good exercise session. On trips, you may find that you use your walks or runs to get to know the new city and that asking for a running route or information on the gym becomes part of your hotel check-in routine. If you find yourself starting these new habits, let yourself enjoy the degree to which you have made an exercise routine part of your life-balancing strategies and your mood regulation efforts. Then go tell your friends about it.

Be sure to congratulate yourself on your accomplishments with this program thus far. Your feeling of success may further motivate you to keep exercising. But remember, you don't have to wait to feel motivated. Go ahead and use exercise to feel good *now*!

Appendix of Forms

Exercise for Mood Log

This log is to help me keep track of my exercise goals for mood by focusing on the importance of exercise several days a week.

Week Number ____

	Day 1 Date: __/__	Day 2 Date: __/__	Day 3 Date: __/__	Day 4 Date: __/__	Day 5 Date: __/__	Day 6 Date: __/__	Day 7 Date: __/__
Day of the week							
Exercise completed (✓)							
Time of day of exercise							
Type of exercise completed							
Intensity (%HR$_{max}$)							
Duration (minutes)							
Pre-exercise Feelings/Mood							
Post-exercise Feelings/Mood							

Exercise for Mood Log

This log is to help me keep track of my exercise goals for mood by focusing on the importance of exercise several days a week.

Week Number _____

	Day 1 Date: __/__	Day 2 Date: __/__	Day 3 Date: __/__	Day 4 Date: __/__	Day 5 Date: __/__	Day 6 Date: __/__	Day 7 Date: __/__
Day of the week							
Exercise completed (✓)							
Time of day of exercise							
Type of exercise completed							
Intensity (%HR$_{max}$)							
Duration (minutes)							
Pre-exercise Feelings/Mood							
Post-exercise Feelings/Mood							

Exercise for Mood Log

This log is to help me keep track of my exercise goals for mood by focusing on the importance of exercise several days a week.

Week Number _____

	Day 1 Date: __/__	Day 2 Date: __/__	Day 3 Date: __/__	Day 4 Date: __/__	Day 5 Date: __/__	Day 6 Date: __/__	Day 7 Date: __/__
Day of the week							
Exercise completed (✓)							
Time of day of exercise							
Type of exercise completed							
Intensity (%HR$_{max}$)							
Duration (minutes)							
Pre-exercise Feelings/Mood							
Post-exercise Feelings/Mood							

Exercise for Mood Log

This log is to help me keep track of my exercise goals for mood by focusing on the importance of exercise several days a week.

Week Number _____

	Day 1 Date: __/__	Day 2 Date: __/__	Day 3 Date: __/__	Day 4 Date: __/__	Day 5 Date: __/__	Day 6 Date: __/__	Day 7 Date: __/__
Day of the week							
Exercise completed (✓)							
Time of day of exercise							
Type of exercise completed							
Intensity (%HR_{max})							
Duration (minutes)							
Pre-exercise Feelings/Mood							
Post-exercise Feelings/Mood							

Exercise for Mood Log

This log is to help me keep track of my exercise goals for mood by focusing on the importance of exercise several days a week.

Week Number _____

	Day 1 Date: ___/___	Day 2 Date: ___/___	Day 3 Date: ___/___	Day 4 Date: ___/___	Day 5 Date: ___/___	Day 6 Date: ___/___	Day 7 Date: ___/___
Day of the week							
Exercise completed (✓)							
Time of day of exercise							
Type of exercise completed							
Intensity (%HR$_{max}$)							
Duration (minutes)							
Pre-exercise Feelings/Mood							
Post-exercise Feelings/Mood							

Exercise for Mood Log

This log is to help me keep track of my exercise goals for mood by focusing on the importance of exercise several days a week.

Week Number _____

	Day 1 Date: ___/___	Day 2 Date: ___/___	Day 3 Date: ___/___	Day 4 Date: ___/___	Day 5 Date: ___/___	Day 6 Date: ___/___	Day 7 Date: ___/___
Day of the week							
Exercise completed (✓)							
Time of day of exercise							
Type of exercise completed							
Intensity (%HR$_{max}$)							
Duration (minutes)							
Pre-exercise Feelings/Mood							
Post-exercise Feelings/Mood							

Exercise Planning Worksheet

My exercise schedule for this week is as follows:

Monday	Tuesday	Wednesday	Thursday
Activity: _____	Activity: _____	Activity: _____	Activity: _____
Intensity: _____	Intensity: _____	Intensity: _____	Intensity: _____
Duration: _____	Duration: _____	Duration: _____	Duration: _____

Friday	Saturday	Sunday	**SUMMARY**
Activity: _____	Activity: _____	Activity: _____	**Intensity:** _____
Intensity: _____	Intensity: _____	Intensity: _____	**Duration:** _____
Duration: _____	Duration: _____	Duration: _____	**Frequency:** _____

Anticipated barriers	*Possible solutions*
1.	1.
	2.
	3.
2.	1.
	2.
	3.

Exercise Planning Worksheet

My exercise schedule for this week is as follows:

Monday	**Tuesday**	**Wednesday**	**Thursday**
Activity: _____	Activity: _____	Activity: _____	Activity: _____
Intensity: _____	Intensity: _____	Intensity: _____	Intensity: _____
Duration: _____	Duration: _____	Duration: _____	Duration: _____
Friday	**Saturday**	**Sunday**	**SUMMARY**
Activity: _____	Activity: _____	Activity: _____	**Intensity:** _____
Intensity: _____	Intensity: _____	Intensity: _____	**Duration:** _____
Duration: _____	Duration: _____	Duration: _____	**Frequency:** _____

Anticipated barriers	*Possible solutions*
1.	1.
	2.
	3.
2.	1.
	2.
	3.

Exercise Planning Worksheet

My exercise schedule for this week is as follows:

Monday	**Tuesday**	**Wednesday**	**Thursday**
Activity: _____	Activity: _____	Activity: _____	Activity: _____
Intensity: _____	Intensity: _____	Intensity: _____	Intensity: _____
Duration: _____	Duration: _____	Duration: _____	Duration: _____
Friday	**Saturday**	**Sunday**	**SUMMARY**
Activity: _____	Activity: _____	Activity: _____	**Intensity:** _____
Intensity: _____	Intensity: _____	Intensity: _____	**Duration:** _____
Duration: _____	Duration: _____	Duration: _____	**Frequency:** _____

Anticipated barriers	*Possible solutions*
1.	1.
	2.
	3.
2.	1.
	2.
	3.

Exercise Planning Worksheet

My exercise schedule for this week is as follows:

Monday	**Tuesday**	**Wednesday**	**Thursday**
Activity: _____	Activity: _____	Activity: _____	Activity: _____
Intensity: _____	Intensity: _____	Intensity: _____	Intensity: _____
Duration: _____	Duration: _____	Duration: _____	Duration: _____

Friday	**Saturday**	**Sunday**	**SUMMARY**
Activity: _____	Activity: _____	Activity: _____	**Intensity:** _____
Intensity: _____	Intensity: _____	Intensity: _____	**Duration:** _____
Duration: _____	Duration: _____	Duration: _____	**Frequency:** _____

Anticipated barriers	*Possible solutions*
1.	1.
	2.
	3.
2.	1.
	2.
	3.

Exercise Planning Worksheet

My exercise schedule for this week is as follows:

Monday	**Tuesday**	**Wednesday**	**Thursday**
Activity: _____	Activity: _____	Activity: _____	Activity: _____
Intensity: _____	Intensity: _____	Intensity: _____	Intensity: _____
Duration: _____	Duration: _____	Duration: _____	Duration: _____

Friday	**Saturday**	**Sunday**	**SUMMARY**
Activity: _____	Activity: _____	Activity: _____	**Intensity:** _____
Intensity: _____	Intensity: _____	Intensity: _____	**Duration:** _____
Duration: _____	Duration: _____	Duration: _____	**Frequency:** _____

Anticipated barriers	*Possible solutions*
1.	1.
	2.
	3.
2.	1.
	2.
	3.

Exercise Planning Worksheet

My exercise schedule for this week is as follows:

Monday	**Tuesday**	**Wednesday**	**Thursday**
Activity: _____	Activity: _____	Activity: _____	Activity: _____
Intensity: _____	Intensity: _____	Intensity: _____	Intensity: _____
Duration: _____	Duration: _____	Duration: _____	Duration: _____
Friday	**Saturday**	**Sunday**	**SUMMARY**
Activity: _____	Activity: _____	Activity: _____	**Intensity:** _____
Intensity: _____	Intensity: _____	Intensity: _____	**Duration:** _____
Duration: _____	Duration: _____	Duration: _____	**Frequency:** _____

Anticipated barriers	*Possible solutions*
1.	1.
	2.
	3.
2.	1.
	2.
	3.

Daily Schedule Planner

	Morning	Mid-Day	Afternoon	Evening
Monday				
Tuesday				
Wednesday				
Thursday				
Friday				
Saturday				
Sunday				

Daily Schedule Planner

	Morning	Mid-Day	Afternoon	Evening
Monday				
Tuesday				
Wednesday				
Thursday				
Friday				
Saturday				
Sunday				

Daily Schedule Planner

	Morning	Mid-Day	Afternoon	Evening
Monday				
Tuesday				
Wednesday				
Thursday				
Friday				
Saturday				
Sunday				

Daily Schedule Planner

	Morning	Mid-Day	Afternoon	Evening
Monday				
Tuesday				
Wednesday				
Thursday				
Friday				
Saturday				
Sunday				

Daily Schedule Planner

	Morning	Mid-Day	Afternoon	Evening
Monday				
Tuesday				
Wednesday				
Thursday				
Friday				
Saturday				
Sunday				

Daily Schedule Planner

	Morning	Mid-Day	Afternoon	Evening
Monday				
Tuesday				
Wednesday				
Thursday				
Friday				
Saturday				
Sunday				

Exercise Practice Log for Panic-Related Concerns

Date of Exercise: _____

What sensations did you experience during your exercise?

_____

_____

_____

How intense were the sensations during your workout (0–100)?

Beginning   :

Half-way   :

Toward the end   :

What was your anxiety level throughout the session (0–100)?

Beginning   :

Half-way   :

Toward the end   :

What were the consequences of the sensations that you experienced?

_____

_____

_____

How did these consequences differ from the fears you had of these sensations due to your panic disorder?

_____

_____

_____

What do you want to tell yourself about these sensations now?

_____

_____

_____

_____

Exercise Practice Log for Panic-Related Concerns

Date of Exercise: _____

What sensations did you experience during your exercise?

_____

_____

_____

How intense were the sensations during your workout (0–100)?

Beginning :

Half-way :

Toward the end :

What was your anxiety level throughout the session (0–100)?

Beginning :

Half-way :

Toward the end :

What were the consequences of the sensations that you experienced?

_____

_____

_____

How did these consequences differ from the fears you had of these sensations due to your panic disorder?

_____

_____

_____

What do you want to tell yourself about these sensations now?

_____

_____

_____

_____

Exercise Practice Log for Panic-Related Concerns

Date of Exercise: _____

What sensations did you experience during your exercise?

_____

_____

_____

How intense were the sensations during your workout (0–100)?

Beginning   :

Half-way   :

Toward the end   :

What was your anxiety level throughout the session (0–100)?

Beginning   :

Half-way   :

Toward the end   :

What were the consequences of the sensations that you experienced?

_____

_____

_____

How did these consequences differ from the fears you had of these sensations due to your panic disorder?

_____

_____

_____

What do you want to tell yourself about these sensations now?

_____

_____

_____

_____

Exercise Practice Log for Panic-Related Concerns

Date of Exercise: _____

What sensations did you experience during your exercise?

_____

_____

_____

How intense were the sensations during your workout (0–100)?

Beginning   :

Half-way   :

Toward the end   :

What was your anxiety level throughout the session (0–100)?

Beginning   :

Half-way   :

Toward the end   :

What were the consequences of the sensations that you experienced?

_____

_____

_____

How did these consequences differ from the fears you had of these sensations due to your panic disorder?

_____

_____

_____

What do you want to tell yourself about these sensations now?

_____

_____

_____

_____

Exercise Practice Log for Panic-Related Concerns

Date of Exercise: _____

What sensations did you experience during your exercise?

_____

_____

_____

How intense were the sensations during your workout (0–100)?

Beginning   :

Half-way   :

Toward the end   :

What was your anxiety level throughout the session (0–100)?

Beginning   :

Half-way   :

Toward the end   :

What were the consequences of the sensations that you experienced?

_____

_____

_____

How did these consequences differ from the fears you had of these sensations due to your panic disorder?

_____

_____

_____

What do you want to tell yourself about these sensations now?

_____

_____

_____

_____

Exercise Practice Log for Panic-Related Concerns

Date of Exercise: _____

What sensations did you experience during your exercise?

_____

_____

_____

How intense were the sensations during your workout (0–100)?

Beginning   :

Half-way   :

Toward the end   :

What was your anxiety level throughout the session (0–100)?

Beginning   :

Half-way   :

Toward the end   :

What were the consequences of the sensations that you experienced?

_____

_____

_____

How did these consequences differ from the fears you had of these sensations due to your panic disorder?

_____

_____

_____

What do you want to tell yourself about these sensations now?

_____

_____

_____

_____

Monthly Exercise Log

Exercise session	Exercise completed	Duration and intensity	Notes and plans
1			
2			
3			
4			
5			
6			
7			
8			
9			
10			
11			
12			
13			
14			
15			
16			
Bonus			
Bonus			
Bonus			

Comments on the month: _____

Special goals or plans for the next month: _____

Monthly Exercise Log

Exercise session	Exercise completed	Duration and intensity	Notes and plans
1			
2			
3			
4			
5			
6			
7			
8			
9			
10			
11			
12			
13			
14			
15			
16			
Bonus			
Bonus			
Bonus			

Comments on the month: _____

Special goals or plans for the next month: _____

Monthly Exercise Log

Exercise session	Exercise completed	Duration and intensity	Notes and plans
1			
2			
3			
4			
5			
6			
7			
8			
9			
10			
11			
12			
13			
14			
15			
16			
Bonus			
Bonus			
Bonus			

Comments on the month: _____

Special goals or plans for the next month: _____

Monthly Exercise Log

Exercise session	Exercise completed	Duration and intensity	Notes and plans
1			
2			
3			
4			
5			
6			
7			
8			
9			
10			
11			
12			
13			
14			
15			
16			
Bonus			
Bonus			
Bonus			

Comments on the month: _____

Special goals or plans for the next month: _____

Monthly Exercise Log

Exercise session	Exercise completed	Duration and intensity	Notes and plans
1			
2			
3			
4			
5			
6			
7			
8			
9			
10			
11			
12			
13			
14			
15			
16			
Bonus			
Bonus			
Bonus			

Comments on the month: _____

Special goals or plans for the next month: _____

Monthly Exercise Log

Exercise session	Exercise completed	Duration and intensity	Notes and plans
1			
2			
3			
4			
5			
6			
7			
8			
9			
10			
11			
12			
13			
14			
15			
16			
Bonus			
Bonus			
Bonus			

Comments on the month: _____

Special goals or plans for the next month: _____

CPSIA information can be obtained
at www.ICGtesting.com
Printed in the USA
BVOW04s1632130917
494709BV00007B/34/P

9 780195 382266